BUFFALO
GOOD NEIGHBORS,
GREAT ARCHITECTURE

CONCRETE ELEVATOR. One of Buffalo's newer grain elevators was built of concrete rather than wood.

THE MAKING OF AMERICA

BUFFALO
GOOD NEIGHBORS,
GREAT ARCHITECTURE

NANCY BLUMENSTALK MINGUS

ARCADIA
PUBLISHING

Copyright © 2003 by Nancy Blumenstalk Mingus
ISBN 978-0-7385-2449-8

Published by Arcadia Publishing,
Charleston SC, Chicago IL, Portsmouth NH, San Francisco CA

Printed in the United States

Library of Congress control number: 2003110666

For all general information contact Arcadia Publishing at:
Telephone 843-853-2070
Fax 843-853-0044
E-Mail sales@arcadiapublishing.com
For customer service and orders:
Toll-Free 1-888-313-2665

Visit us on the Internet at www.arcadiapublishing.com

CONTENTS

Acknowledgments   6

Introduction   7

1.   What's in a Name?   9

2.   Early Settlement   13

3.   Destruction and Rebuilding   23

4.   Erie Canal Days   31

5.   Civil War Looms and Passes   49

6.   Glory Days   103

7.   Pan-American Era   111

8.   World War I Era   123

9.   World War II   133

10. The Fall of the Queen City   139

11. The City Today   151

Bibliography   157

Index   159

ACKNOWLEDGMENTS

Several people have helped me with this project, knowingly and unknowingly. Cynthia VanNess, Chuck LaChuisa, Chris Andrle, Chris Brown, Nancy Piatkowski, Mike Rizzo, George Richmond, and the rest of the gang on the Buffalo History list all helped me iron out conflicting facts. Cynthia and Chuck also provided me with valuable additional references; my daughter, Paige, helped by scanning most of the images; and my editors, Jim Kempert and Barbie Langston, answered my myriad of questions with the patience of a saint. Thanks to you all.

INTRODUCTION

Buffalo, New York has been known by a variety of nicknames over the years. Queen City of the Lakes, Nickel City, and City of Good Neighbors are the three most common. Of these, I believe the Queen City is most appropriate for this history, for while the neighborly attitudes of the citizens are still superior to those in many cities, our place in the country's history deserves the Queen City sobriquet. This section introduces you to the Queen City, its explosive growth in the late nineteenth and early twentieth centuries, and the social and cultural events that shaped the lives of its residents over the past two centuries.

CITY OVERVIEW

Buffalo, New York is located at the eastern end of Lake Erie in Western New York, approximately 300 miles due west of New York's capital city, Albany, and 400 miles northwest of New York City. Set at the mouth of the Buffalo Creek (now generally known as the Buffalo River), the city is in a prime strategic location, which lead to settlement of the area in the late 1700s. At its peak, the city was the eighth largest in the United States, and still today it is the second largest city in New York State.

Buffalo is approximately 42 square miles with about 10 miles of waterfront on Lake Erie and the Niagara River. Its geographic coordinates are 42°50'47" north latitude and 79°22'37" west longitude. Despite popular belief outside the city, the average temperature is a balmy 48 degrees. Winter temperatures average in the mid-20s, while summer temperatures average in the 70s. More importantly, in its recorded history there has never been a day with temperatures in the 100s. The lake provides constant cooling summer breezes. This climate is what attracted settlers to the area in the first place.

If any city in the United States can claim to have made America, it is Buffalo. Throughout the 1800s and into the early 1900s, Buffalo was a major connection point between New York City and other East Coast cities and the Midwest cities of Detroit and Chicago. The Erie Canal, opened in 1825, represented the first phase of transportation through the city, and by the mid 1800s, Buffalo was also a major railroad center. The West and South could not have been opened without these transportation venues.

In fact, it was a Buffalo invention that allowed settlement of hostile hot regions. Willis Carrier, while working in the Buffalo Forge plant, created the first device known to the world today as an air conditioner. Other Buffalo firsts include the grain elevator and the implantable pacemaker. And, of course, Buffalo wings.

Two U.S. presidents, Millard Fillmore and Grover Cleveland, were from Buffalo. Fillmore retired here after his presidency and is buried in the historic Forest Lawn Cemetery. In 1901, Buffalo hosted the world at the Pan-American Exhibition, then led the mourners after President McKinley was assassinated here.

Buffalo has a rich architectural heritage. In fact, it is one of only four cities in the world with extant buildings designed by architectural history's "Holy Trinity" of Frank Lloyd Wright, Louis Sullivan, and H.H. Richardson. It is home to the first comprehensive park system in the country and to the prototype of the now destroyed World Trade Center.

While the declining years of the twentieth century also brought a major decline in the city, Buffalo started to rebound in the 1990s and is now on a slow climb back up.

BOOK OVERVIEW

Such a slender volume can't possibly cover everything in our three centuries of history, so the following chapters will highlight the major events and people of their times. Hopefully, this will give you the flavor of the city during the various eras and also wet your appetite for more in-depth research on the history of our great city.

In doing the research for this book, I discovered many discrepancies in the primary and secondary resources usually considered the ultimate works in their areas. In cases where there is no clear right or wrong in the facts or stories, I've chosen to report the various versions. In other cases, I've simply picked the one that seems most reliable. Those of you who know of additional reliable and contradictory sources, feel free to let me know.

Enjoy.

Chapter One

WHAT'S IN A NAME?

Before we can talk about the evolution of the city of Buffalo itself, we need to address the great name debate. For most cities, the naming is a historic event, well documented and oft recited, but this is not the case with Buffalo. Most residents know some of the popular theories, yet the derivation of the name continues to be a discussion point among residents and historians.

The earliest documented use of the name Buffalo Creek was in an essay called "Narrative of the Captivity of the Gilbert Family," dating either to 1780 or 1782. The 1784 treaty with the Iroquois Confederacy also uses the name Buffalo Creek, as do two other treaties in 1789 and 1794.

No one argues that the original settlement, and later the city, was named for the creek on which it was located, but how that creek got its name is hotly disputed. The most common theory is that the creek was named for the wild buffalo that watered on it and ate at the nearby salt lick. While several "experts" in the late 1800s tried to show this wasn't possible by proving that buffalo never roamed in the area, their arguments were unconvincing in the face of other evidence.

According to William Ketchum, who delivered an 1863 address on this subject, several early travelers to Lake Erie's south shore, including LaSalle in 1680 and La Hontan in 1687–1688, noted the buffalo roaming in the great meadows here. Says LaSalle, "The wild bulls are grown somewhat scarce, since the Illinois have been at war with their neighbors (the Iroquois), for now all parties are continually a-hunting them." And according to La Hontan, "At the bottom of the lake . . . we find wild beeves, upon the banks of two rivers that disembogue into it without cataracts or rapid currents." A third traveler, Charlevoix, in 1721 notes, "I cannot say there is such a plenty of game in the woods, but I know that on the south side of the lake, there are vast herds of wild cattle."

So it is likely that buffalo did in fact roam here until the mid 1700s. However, this doesn't mean this is where the creek got its name, because settlers would not have known of the earlier existence of buffalo when naming their settlement.

Another common theory is that the creek's name came from mispronunciation or misinterpretation of an Indian word. This seems unlikely because, though no one can agree on the exact Indian word or its pronunciation, it is overwhelmingly clear that the translation meant "place of the basswood," for the dense basswood lining the creek. And the words themselves—"Te-u-shu-wa," "Te-osah-way," and "Do-sh-wa"—don't lend themselves to be mispronounced "Buffalo," so it is doubtful the name is a derivation of an Indian word.

If there is an Indian connection, it is more likely related to the next theory, which postulates that an Indian named Buffalo lived on the creek, prompting the early non-natives to call the stream "Buffalo's Creek." This Seneca was said to have been a member of the Wolf clan and called "De-gi-yah-goh," or "Buffalo" by his tribe. He built a basswood bark cabin by the creek and fished there and became known as the chief fisherman for the Seneca. Captain Daniel Dobbins, in recounting a 1795 conversation with Buffalo resident Cornelius Winney, says this, "He assigned the reason for this sobriquet that the old Indian was a large, square framed man, with stooped shoulders and a large bushy head which . . . made him resemble a Buffalo." This could very well be the source of the name, since Indians did use animal names for themselves and not usually their places. It would also explain how the name got passed down among both the native and non-native settlers.

Although several theories involve Indian names, there are an equal number that revolve around the early French explorers. These French-based theories include that the name comes from the French words *beau fleuve*, meaning beautiful river, or *boeuf a leau*, meaning oxen or cattle at the water. Either of these are certainly possible, though not likely, only because these theories don't surface in discussions until much later in the city's history. The theories mentioned earlier have been circulating as early as 1825, while the two above were not mentioned in William Ketchum's 1863 "The Name of Buffalo" address to the Buffalo Historical Society. This presumably means they hadn't surfaced by then or had been dismissed as unlikely.

Perhaps the most interesting story comes from Sheldon Ball, who in 1825 combined the roaming Buffalo and French explorer threads in this amusing tale:

> At a period long before its first settlement, a party of French, bound up the Lake, in a bateau, sought shelter in the Creek; being short of provisions, despatched a hunting party, who, while in search of game, fell in with a horse, (belonging, probably, to a neighboring tribe of Indians,) that was soon made a sacrifice, by the hungry huntsmen, dressed, and taken to their companions, with the deceptive information, that it was the flesh of a Buffaloe, which they had killed. Hence came the name of Buffalo Creek, and consequently the Village.

While this is an entertaining anecdote, it is probably fiction. Other similar "slaughtered horse called buffalo" stories abound, but all have the same drawbacks. Although the people involved in the stories might have jokingly referred to the settlement as "Buffalo" afterward, how would that name have been passed on to subsequent visitors?

The most likely derivation of the name, then, is that of an Indian named Buffalo. Since he was apparently quite a memorable man, his name would be passed down by anyone coming to the area and meeting him, even long before any written records existed. Says N.L. Strong in a letter to Ketchum regarding his address to the historical society, "From all the facts and circumstances, I think it is due to the truth of history to say that it is the Indian 'Buffalo' to whom the creek and finally the city owes its name. Little fame will the poor Indian reap from it; but to the animal buffalo from which doubtless he derived his name, the millions in all time to come will award that honor."

Whatever the origin of the name, by 1791, the residents in the settlement and visitors to the area were using the name Buffalo. This may be because at least one early resident, Martin Middaugh, had moved here from Pennsylvania, which also has a Buffalo Creek, and he was content to perpetuate the name, but the record does not show any definitive data. Whether after the animal, the Indian, myths, earlier settlements, or French or Indian words, Buffalo continued to be the name, despite the fact that the Dutch owners dubbed the city "New Amsterdam" in 1800.

With a brief overview and the questions of name behind us, we can move on to exploring the rich history of the city.

Chapter Two

EARLY SETTLEMENT

The Buffalo area was home to various Indian tribes well into the late 1700s, but European explorers and traders started visiting the area in the 1600s. The first known great ship on Lake Erie was built north of the city and entered the lake near Buffalo in the late 1600s. By the late 1700s, the area was a thriving trade hub. From the early settlement of the area to the city layout designed by Joseph Ellicott in 1801–1802, few could guess at the subsequent growth.

EARLY RESIDENTS

Just as with the naming of the area, there is considerable debate over when Buffalo was first visited and settled by non–Native Americans. As early as 1612 French explorers, trappers, and missionaries were active along the St. Lawrence River and were likely active in the Buffalo region as well. During this time, several tribes of Native Americans, including the Eries, the Algonquins, the Kahquahs (or "Neuter Indians"), and the original five tribes of the Iroquois Confederacy, including the Seneca, occupied the land. The Kahquahs were a peace-loving people noted for getting along harmoniously with the neighboring and more hostile tribes. Unfortunately, the harmony did not last and somewhere during the years 1640–1655, the Neuters and Eries were annihilated or driven off by the Seneca. The Seneca then occupied the land until the late 1700s, although the French continued to visit regularly.

In 1669, the French nobleman Rene Robert Cavelier de la Salle came with two others to explore the western New York wilderness. The following year, two Sulpician priests from Montreal, Francois Dollier de Casson and his companion Rene-Francois Brehant de Galinee, traveled here on their way to Sault St. Marie. Near Port Dover, Ontario (and perhaps also near Detroit), they claimed possession of the "lands of the lake named Erie" in the name of France and the Catholic Church by erecting a cross. Galinee also created one of the first detailed maps of the Great Lakes west of Lake Ontario.

La Salle returned to the area with a larger party in early 1678 and camped on the Niagara River at Lake Ontario. He was sent there by the Duke of Frontenac, who was the governor of New France (Canada) from 1672 to 1682 and again in 1689–1693. Accompanying La Salle were three priests, including Father Hennepin, who became the party's scribe and the first to publicize the majesty of Niagara Falls. The group's improvements to this area were later incorporated into what would become today's Fort Niagara.

According to Hennepin's accounts, La Salle then moved to a spot above Niagara Falls at Cayuga Creek, presently the La Salle area of the city of Niagara Falls. Here he constructed a ship he dubbed the *Griffon* after the mythical beast on Governor Frontenac's family coat of arms. The ship was nearly finished in May 1679 and was launched early, as the Senecas were threatening to burn it. From relative safety now anchored in the river, the ship was completed. La Salle and his party set sail upriver to the section of Buffalo now known as Black Rock. But weather conditions and a swift current kept the ship from traveling any further until August 7, when the breeze finally picked up and they were able to enter Lake Erie. It is said that the *Griffon* was referred to as "The Great (or Big) Canoe" by the Indian natives who viewed it. With its cargo capacity of about 60 tons, crew size of 33–34, and artillery load of seven cannon, the *Griffon* became the first ship to sail Lake Erie.

In September 1687, another French nobleman, Louis Armond de Lom d'Ares, Baron de Lahontan, traveled to the area with the Marquis Denonville, the newly appointed governor of Canada. Lahontan proposed to Denonville that a fort be built in the Buffalo area and went so far as marking on his map "Fort Suppose." That same year Denonville did rebuild La Salle's ruined fort at the present Fort Niagara, but no records of a Fort Suppose have been located.

It would be nearly 70 years before anything resembling a fort would be built in Buffalo. In 1758, Daniel-Marie Joncaire Sieur de Chabert (also called Clausonne to differentiate him from his father and elder brother) built a trading post on the south side of Buffalo Creek, near the foot of present day Michigan Street. The post was evacuated in 1759 in anticipation of a British arrival. In 1719 or 1721, Joncaire (though which one is not always clear) had built a similar trading post near Lewiston and another near Niagara Falls in 1750. The stone chimney from the Niagara Falls post is still extant in that city.

Although they did develop forts and trading posts, the French explorers did not build permanent residences in the area. Depending on the source you choose to believe, this honor fell to Cornelius Winney (or Winne), who built a home in Buffalo somewhere between 1789 and 1791. Cornelius Winney was an Indian trader who had built a house on the east side of Washington at Quay, according to Colonel

Early Settlement

Thomas Proctor, who visited the area in March of 1791. Other sources say that Martin Middaugh and his son-in-law Ezekial (Ezekiel) Lane were the first permanent residents, arriving prior to 1791. Still other sources suggest that neither Winney nor Middaugh can lay claim to first resident because that honor fell to a tavern operator/ Indian trader named Joseph Hodge. Hodge is also known as Joe Hodges and "Black Joe," and he traded here with the Indians into the early nineteenth century before moving away. According to some, Proctor also notes Hodge as a partner of Winney's and a resident since 1771.

Still others credit Captain William Johnston (Johnson) as being the first resident, settling in Buffalo Creek *c.* 1780–1781. These individuals may have been here prior to 1790, but when the first census was conducted that same year, there were no residents listed in this area. In his 1865 account of the history of the Buffalo Post Office, Nathan Hall explains this discrepancy: ". . . it is probable that the deputy marshal did not visit this locality, as neither Winney the Indian trader, nor Johnston the Indian agent and interpreter, is named; although it is probable that both of them resided here. Winney, it is quite certain, was here in 1791, and it is supposed came about 1784." Unfortunately, only General Amos Hall, who served as deputy marshal for this area, knows for sure if he visited Buffalo or not.

There is no dispute, however, that by 1795, when La Rochefoucault Liancourt visited Buffalo, there were already at least four houses belonging to Winney, Johnston, Lane, and Middaugh. According to Joseph Landon, who was a member of a 1796 surveying party, Jesse Skinner and Hodge were also here. Another source says that Asa Ransom was a resident by 1796, as were John Palmer and Sylvanus Maybee by 1798.

So who were these valiant settlers of western New York's wilderness?

Cornelius Winney was most likely the first European to settle in the area. Proctor notes he was in the area in 1791 and another traveler, Hinds Chamberlain, also mentions Winney in his 1792 journals, saying, "His building stood first as you descend from the high ground. He had rum, whiskey, Indian knives, trinkets, etc. His house was full of Indians." Winney was Dutch and moved here from the settlements in the Hudson Valley, most likely from the Fishkill area which was once called "Fish Kills." He apparently left the area around 1798.

Joseph Hodge was a former slave who had been captured by the Seneca Indians during the Revolutionary War. He was released in 1784, married a Seneca woman, and they settled in the area sometime prior to 1792. They lived in a log cabin near Winney. Since Hodge was fluent in the Seneca tongue, he was an active Indian trader and sometimes functioned as interpreter, too. In 1796, he was hired as a guide and interpreter for Moses Cleaveland's surveying party working west of Buffalo to Conneaut Creek near present day Cleveland, Ohio. Some reports say that Hodge and his wife later moved to the Cattaraugus Creek Reservation, where he died, yet others claim he moved on to Canada. Regardless of where he went, he was no longer in Buffalo by 1810. There are also rumors that Hodge was involved in the Underground Railroad activity in Buffalo, but this isn't likely unless it was in the very early 1800s and not the more traditional Underground Railroad time frame.

Martin Middaugh was a German cooper who moved to Buffalo after living in Canada near Fort Erie. Although some accounts say Middaugh was Dutch, others claim he was actually from German-Pennsylvanian stock, i.e. Pennsylvania Dutch. He could speak fluently with the local Iroquois and originally settled on the south side of the creek, moving next to Johnston later. Says Landon:

> In 1796 I was one of the party of surveyors that came on to survey what was then call'd New Connecticut in Ohio. In June we came into the Buffalo Creek with our boats and picked our camp on the bank of the creek just below the mouth of the Little Buffalo. We remained here some 10 or 12 days. At that time there was old Mr. Medaw [Middaugh] with his son-in-law Mr. Lane and his family; they lived in a log house a little north of Exchange Street, near the tannery.

Others have described the building Middaugh and Lane occupied as a "double log house" located a little west of present day Main and north of Exchange. Middaugh continued to live in Buffalo through its early village years and until his death in 1822 (or 1825). According to some accounts, Lane lived here until 1848, dying at the age of 102, and they credit his son born in 1786 as being the first child born in Buffalo.

William Johnston visited the area around 1780 as a lieutenant in the military and later returned, most speculate, around 1793. By that time he was called Captain Johnston. He married a women from the Seneca village, bought land, built five buildings including a sawmill, and raised his family here. He owned about 40 acres of land running from Seneca Street south to the Little Buffalo Creek and to a line east from Washington. His home was half log and half frame. He established the first cemetery in Buffalo on his land near what is now Washington and Exchange. He lived here until 1807, when he died and was buried in the family cemetery.

Little is known about Jesse Skinner, other than that in 1796 he was operating an inn/tavern in Buffalo. He later purchased land from the Holland Land Company in 1805, but moved to Wood County, Ohio in 1810.

John Palmer ran a tavern in a two story log building owned by Johnston. This was purported to be the first tavern in Buffalo. Arriving somewhere around 1798, he was gone again by *c.* 1802.

Asa Ransom moved to Buffalo from Massachusetts via Geneva, where he'd married and started a family. He chose to live at what would become Main and Terrace, building a log home there. In 1797, his wife gave birth to a second daughter, who is credited in some accounts with being the first non–Native-American child born in Buffalo. Ransom moved to Clarence in 1799, and an inn bearing his name still operates there.

ELLICOTT AND THE HOLLAND PURCHASE

While these early residents were building homes and forts, the land actually belonged to the Massachusetts Bay Province, as granted to it by King Charles I in 1628. This charter of land approximately 150 miles wide from north to south extended from the Atlantic clear to the Pacific. In 1788, the now state of Massachusetts sold its land in New York State to two businessmen, Oliver Phelps and Nathaniel Gorham. This amounted to about 6 million acres for a price of $1 million. Unfortunately, Phelps and Gorham did not keep up the payments to Massachusetts and the state later resold the land in five tracks to Robert Morris from Philadelphia.

During 1792 and 1793, Morris resold the four westernmost tracks— encompassing all the land in western New York west of the Genesee River and north of the Pennsylvania border—to agents for a group of Holland businessmen. This group is generally referred to as the Holland Land Corporation or Holland Land Company, although it is also speculated that no such formal company ever existed. These four tracks of land became known as "The Holland Purchase," and the company set up western New York headquarters in Batavia, New York, which was one of the earliest settlements in the area, approximately 35 miles northeast of Buffalo.

Unfortunately for Morris and the Holland Land Company, because of New York State's treaty with the Iroquois, settlers could not occupy the land without Indian permission. In Geneseo, New York, Morris, with the help of interpreters Horatio Jones and Jasper Parrish, negotiated with the Seneca. The Treaty of Big Tree was signed in September 1797, selling to Morris all the Holland Purchase land except 337 square miles to be divided into ten Indian reservations. What Morris ended up paying Red Jacket, the leader of the Seneca, is also debated. Some sources say the sum was $10,000, while others say it was $100,000. Either way, one-third of a cent to 3¢ per acre was still very low, even with the lower costs of the times.

Shortly after the land was purchased from the Indians, the Holland Land Company began subdividing it into smaller units of about 120 acres, which it resold to men willing to build taverns on the property. To further encourage settlement, the company built or funded roads, bridges, and mills. The first road capable of wagon traffic was built from the East Transit Line to Buffalo in 1798 along an old Indian trail.

That same year, the owners of the Holland Land Company were Wilhelm Willink, Wilhelm Willink Jr., Jan Willink, Jan Willink Jr., Nicholas Van Staphorst, Jan Gabriel Van Staphorst, Roelif Van Staphorst Jr., Pieter Van Eeghen, Hendrick Vollenhoven, Cornelius Vollenhoven, Rutger Van Schimmelpennick, Henrick Seye, and Pieter Stadnitski. Serving at that time as general agent for the group was Theophilus Cazenove, who was replaced in 1799 by Paul Busti, who remained general agent until 1824.

In 1797, this group had hired Joseph Ellicott to survey all the lands in western New York. The survey began in early 1798. Working with a team of 130–150 men, primarily surveyors and their assistants, Ellicott took nearly three years to thoroughly survey the land. The survey cost $71,000. In the process, to aid in the accuracy of the measurements, Ellicott developed the modern 1-foot ruler still in use today. He did this by gathering a variety of measuring devices then in use, averaging their lengths and then developing an "average-length" ruler. Ellicott's younger brother Benjamin also designed and built the "transit" surveying device used in the survey. This device is used to measure distances based on star positions when surveying in the thick woods. A new one was needed for this survey because the only other one known in the country was being used by the elder Ellicott, Andrew, in a survey he was conducting in Florida.

Joseph Ellicott was a Quaker, born in Bucks County, Pennsylvania in 1760, six years after brother Andrew. The three boys were taught math and science, especially the science of surveying. After the western New York survey work was completed in 1800, Joseph and Benjamin became sales agents for the subset of land encompassing the current counties of Erie and Niagara. Since Joseph and his brother, Andrew, had worked closely with Pierre L'Enfant in the design of Washington, D.C., as part of his new responsibilities, Joseph was tasked with developing a similar plan for Buffalo.

In 1804, the plan was published, creating streets, lots, and circles running north to Chippewa Street, east to Ellicott Street, south to Buffalo Creek, and west to the New York State Indian Reservation Line, which ran from Genesee Street to Morgan Street, delineating one of the reservations created with the Big Tree Treaty. Ellicott called his village "New Amsterdam" in honor of its owners. He also named the major streets after them. What is now the southern portion of Main Street, Ellicott named "Willinks Avenue," while the northern portion was called "Van Staphorst Avenue." Erie Street was called "Vollenhovens Avenue," Niagara Street was named "Schimmelpennicks Avenue," Church Street "Stadnitski," Genesee Street was called "Busti Avenue," and Court Street "Cazenovia Avenue." All of the above name changes were made to their current ones in 1826. Original streets named after Indian tribes were also changed at that time. Washington was changed from Onondaga, Ellicott from Oneida, Franklin from Tuscarora, Pearl from Cayuga, and Exchange from Crow.

Lots in New Amsterdam became available for sale in 1804, and that same year 15 were sold. Since the point was to increase settlement of the village, no one was allowed to buy land on speculation. The lot buyers had to agree to construct a home or business there. As is still the case today, the price of the land lots varied with location. Prime downtown lots went for $135–140 each while lots on Pearl and Chippewa cost $25–45 each. Tavern lots were sold in the outlying areas along the road into Buffalo. These lots were approximately 10 miles apart, which represented then one day's travel. To encourage tavern development, these lots were sold at $2 an acre.

Ellicott purchased for himself village lot number 104, which was 100 acres extending east from Main to present day Jefferson, and north and south from Eagle to Swan. The Main Street section of the lot was arced and Ellicott intended to build his mansion along the arc as many European houses were. When the village leaders decided to straighten Main and remove the curved portion of his lot, however, Ellicott decided to move to Batavia instead. He continued to serve as agent for the Holland Land Company for a total of 20 years. As he aged, however, his mind and health quickly failed. He was placed in the Bloomingdale Asylum in New York City. He committed suicide there in 1826 when he was 66.

COMMUNITY DEVELOPS

When the first taxes in the Holland Purchase were levied in October of 1800, there were but four dwellers taxed. They were William Johnston, Martin Middaugh, Ezekial

BUFFALO

Lane, and John Palmer. The total value of the taxed property was only $2,675, and the total tax levied a mere $4.55. The breakdown among the residents was Johnson, $2,034 for a tax of $3.50; Palmer, $482 for a tax of 72¢; Lane, $114 for a tax of 24¢; and Middaugh, $45 for a mere 9¢ tax.

It was during the early years from 1800 to 1810 that key citizens also came to town. One was Cyrenius Chapin, the first resident doctor/undertaker. Born in Massachusetts in 1769, Chapin learned his practice from his elder brother. He married in 1793, then moved first to Vermont and later to Sangerfield in Oneida County, New York. Not content there either, he originally arrived in Buffalo in 1801. But Chapin couldn't buy any land because Ellicott's survey wasn't finished, so he moved back to Sangerfield. In 1803, he returned to Buffalo, but was unable to purchase suitable housing, so he moved on to Fort Erie, Canada. He stayed in Canada for three years and developed a significant practice, providing him with the funds he needed to establish himself in Buffalo. He returned to the area in 1805 (or 1806), purchased a lot at the corner of Main and Swan for $150, and built his home.

Chapin opened the first drugstore in town and continued to practice medicine both here and in Fort Erie. During the war of 1812, he served as lieutenant colonel in the militia and later was a military surgeon. He lived for a few years in Geneva after the war, returning to his old home and practice in 1818, where he remained until his death in 1838. He was buried in the old cemetery under what is now Old City and County Hall, and his body was one of those disinterred and moved to Forest Lawn when it opened in 1851.

Another key citizen in Buffalo's early years was Erastus Granger. According to a Buffalo Historical Society preface to several Granger speeches:

> . . . Granger reached Buffalo Creek, traveling on horseback, on the 30th of March, 1804, to find it a village of sixteen huts, its streets filled with stumps and its inhabitants the usual class found in a frontier town. It was not even a postoffice, but as part of the agreement he had made with the Government was that a post-office should be located there, he was soon (September 3, 1804), commissioned 'Postmaster at Buffaloe Creek.'

Granger continued to serve as postmaster until 1818. The Buffalo post office played a key role in the War of 1812, as all military communication to Commodore Perry and other military leaders west of Buffalo went first to the Buffalo post office.

Early Settlement

From his arrival until 1812, Granger was also the Collector of the Port for Buffalo. He was appointed county judge in 1807, remained on the bench until 1817, and was a key agent of peace with the Six Nations at the start of the War of 1812. He served as town supervisor from 1816 to 1817. He helped build one of Buffalo's most prominent landmarks—the original Buffalo harbor lighthouse—and his farm known as Flint Hill is now part of Forest Lawn Cemetery.

In 1806, Ebenezer Walden, Buffalo's first lawyer, arrived. Born in Massachusetts in 1777, Walden moved west from Oneida County, where he had been since he graduated from Williams College in 1799. He opened his office on Main Street between Exchange and Seneca, working as a lawyer when possible but also at a variety of odd jobs, as demand for lawyers at that time was low. In 1810, Walden bought land at the corner of Main and Eagle to build a residence and also started accumulating land throughout the village. His home was burned in the war, and in rebuilding it later, he was proud owner of the first brick house in Buffalo. He also helped others in their redevelopment efforts, founded several key companies and organizations, served as a state representative, and went on to become mayor in 1838.

After staying in Ohio at the end of the 1796 Ohio survey, surveyor Joseph Landon returned to Buffalo to live in 1806. He purchased a tavern known then as Crow's Tavern, located at the southwestern corner of Washington and Exchange Streets. Later referred to as the Mansion House, Landon's tavern was the site of many of the most important meetings in the young village's history, including the formation of a school and the first Niagara County Court Session.

It is also Landon who provides us with a rare glimpse of early life in Buffalo. In his 1863 speech to the Buffalo Historical Society, he describes the village when he arrived:

> In 1806 I moved with my family to Buffalo, and purchased the Mansion House property. A man by the name of John Crow kept the tavern there. Capt. Samuel Pratt's house was on the corner of Main and Exchange Streets. He was a merchant and his store was on Exchange Street, adjoining his house. Mr. Louis LeCouteulx lived opposite; he kept an apothecary shop all in the same house.

Landon goes on to describe a merchant named Sylvanus Mabee with a store on Exchange Street and a house at Main and West Seneca Streets, and his clerk, Jack Johnson, who lived with his father, Captain Johnson, at Exchange and Washington. Another man named Palmer lived near Johnson also on Washington, as did a baker named John Despar (or Despard). On an opposite corner of Main and Seneca lived a blacksmith named David Reese whose shop was on the northwest corner. Another blacksmith named Phillips lived on Main near Ebenezer Walden's law office and several other stores and taverns were clustered along in these same blocks.

As more people settled in the area, Buffalo started to develop into a true community. And as community developed, so did the need for community-related resources such as schools, churches, meeting halls, even cemeteries.

What might be considered the first true community building was the school, built in 1807–1808 at Pearl and Swan, on the present site of the Dun Building. Prior to having a separate school building, school sessions were conducted in Martin Middaugh's house by a schoolmaster named Hiram Hanchett. At a meeting at Landon's in March of 1807, the major citizens agreed they needed to build a new structure to house the school. Sometimes referred to as the Little Red Schoolhouse, the small frame building was constructed by local citizens Levi Strong and George Kith, purportedly for $68.50. The first teacher in the new building was said to be a Presbyterian pastor named Samuel Whiting. The school was multi-functional, also being used as a church and community hall.

Other types of cultural groups evolved as the population grew. In 1809, Reverend James Mitchell established a Methodist Episcopal church, although it appears no building was constructed. The Reverend Thaddeus Osgood founded the First Presbyterian Church in February of 1812 and this remains Buffalo's oldest religious organization.

Other early residents included William Robbins, Henry Chapin, Thomas Stewart, Jonas Williams, Robert Kain, Vincent Grant, Thomas Sidwell, Nathaniel W. Seaver, Isaac Rhoads, Samuel Tupper, Asa Chapman, David Mather, Daniel Lewis, Oziel Smith, John White, and Eleazer Hovey. Although little is known about these men, they also contributed to the growth of the city.

With this solid core of citizens and community groups, Buffalo was poised on the brink of greatness, but that was all about to change dramatically.

Chapter Three

DESTRUCTION AND REBUILDING

Because of its prime waterfront location, Buffalo was a prized site in the War of 1812 and was burned by the British in 1813. Nearly all the buildings were destroyed and the newly incorporated village would need another three years to rebuild. The area saw great participation in the war, the devastating effects of the burning, and subsequent rebuilding into the 1820s.

PRELUDE TO WAR

The period from 1804 through 1813 brought great changes to the area. After the village was platted, roads were constructed and taverns were built along the major routes into the village. Settlement expanded not just in Buffalo, but in the surrounding areas, too. In the spring of 1805, the village was declared an official port of entry by the federal government. It was made the county seat of Niagara County in 1808 when Niagara County was formed from Genesee County.

In June of 1808, Augustus Porter, formerly principal surveyor for the Ohio survey, was appointed the first county judge. Shortly thereafter, the Holland Land Company donated land on Washington for the erection of the first courthouse. It was completed in 1809. According to journals from the time, becoming the county seat was a great coup for the village, bringing in both court-related activity during "court week" as well as more settlers.

By that time, according to Landon, there were two taverns, thirteen houses, four stores, one apothecary, one baker, two blacksmiths, one missionary/pastor, one teacher, one doctor, and Granger as postmaster. Says Landon, "The mail was brought through once a week on horseback from Canandaigua." There was a ferry across the creek run by tavern owner Zenas Barker and a road along the edge of the river up to the village of Black Rock.

In 1810, the Town of Buffalo was created from the Town of Clarence and in the spring of 1813, the Village of Buffalo was incorporated. Trustees named at that time were Walden and Chapin as well as Oliver Forward, Eli Hart, and Zenas Barker. Due primarily to the war, the village would be reincorporated in 1816, and again in 1822. Trustees in the 1816 incorporation still included Walden and Forward, with the addition of Heman Potter, Jonas Harrison, Samuel Wilkeson, and Charles Townsend.

But while all this forward progress was happening in western New York, larger, negative forces were at work internationally. There were an increasing number of attacks on Americans by the British, who seized goods, ships, even men, and then pressed them into British service. The American outcry was virtually non-existent at first, but as the seizures continued, they became difficult to ignore. In June 1812, the new U.S. government had had enough and war was declared. The first battles broke out on the Great Lakes near Detroit shortly thereafter.

WAR OF 1812

The same prime waterfront location that made Buffalo an ideal place for settlement also made it a military target, so a military post was created in August of 1812. Known as Fort Tompkins, or Fort Adams, the post was a large earthwork structure set above the river off Niagara Street. The fort, or battery, was the biggest of the eight built at that time, holding seven large guns. It is estimated that as many as 2,000 regular army and militiamen were stationed in Buffalo in the early days of the war, yet all that remains of the fort today is a historic plaque marking the spot.

Although skirmishes were taking place throughout the country, largely in the northern border areas, the first hostile act that had a direct influence on the village was the burning of Newark, now called Niagara-on-the-Lake. By the fall of 1813, a group of Americans under the command of General George McClure had been slowly losing their numbers to desertions. In December of 1813, McClure lost half his men when their enlistment period was over. Discouraged by the turn of events, McClure chose to retreat from Canada and regroup in Fort Niagara. Unfortunately, as they were departing, McClure ordered that the village be burned. In so doing, the Americans left what some estimates say were more than 400 people, primarily women and children, homeless. Several sources say that, although the town was destroyed, no one was injured, but others say that in the bitter Canadian winter weather, more than 100 residents froze to death without shelter. McClure was dismissed for his actions, but that hardly appeased the British.

Retaliation started on December 19 when the 400 men defending Fort Niagara were defeated in a surprise morning attack. The British then moved south to Lewiston and burned it to the ground. Luckily most of the inhabitants had fled, because the Indians killed all who had remained.

Destruction and Rebuilding

On December 30, British forces crossed the river again, landing at a battery north of Buffalo. With only sparse militia forces to protect the battery, the British easily took control and headed to Black Rock. Although Major General Amos Hall had nearly 2,000 men stationed with him in Buffalo, most were not properly prepared to fight, and on the march north to Black Rock, many ran off. By the time they got to Black Rock, only around 600 remained. They were quickly outflanked and most of the rest of the troops fled. As the British burned Black Rock, the cry went up along the way to abandon Buffalo, and many did, heading south toward Hamburg or east toward Williamsville.

But others stayed in a valiant effort to protect their property. One of these was doctor and lieutenant colonel Cyrenius Chapin. Chapin, returning from the defeat at Black Rock, gathered some of the few remaining men, found a large gun, and began firing on the British. But the gun didn't last long, and soon Chapin decided the prudent thing to do was to negotiate a surrender.

His terms were that all public property and armaments would be given to the British in return for the safety of the women and children and private buildings. The British commander agreed to the terms, then promptly ordered the village burned. While Chapin was unable to save the structures, his tactics at least delayed the destruction long enough to allow most of the residents to leave the village. He and Ebenezer Walden were taken prisoner, but Walden managed to escape. Chapin, on the other hand, was transported to Montreal and held for nine months.

When the destruction was over, only two to four buildings remained. The two that positively were still standing were the jail and one home. The jail stood because it was stone. The home was intentionally spared. It belonged to Mrs. Margaret St. John, who actually owned two homes; one large residence on the northeast corner of Washington and Seneca Streets, and another small one on Main north of Church. When the British came to burn her homes, she begged that they be spared. On the first day, they both were, but when the attackers returned a second day, the large home was burned.

One source says that a third stone structure on Washington near Clinton was also spared, while several say that the number remaining was actually four. In the 1869 *Pictorial Fieldbook of the War of 1812*, written by Benson J. Lossing, Lossing claims four structures remained:

> The British and their Indian allies took possession of Buffalo, and
> proceeded to plunder, destroy, and slaughter. Only four buildings were

left standing in the town. These were the jail (built of stone), the frame of a barn, Reese's blacksmith-shop, and the dwelling of Mrs. St. John, a resolute woman, who, more fortunate than her neighbor, Mrs. Lovejoy (who was murdered and burnt in her own house), saved her own life and her property.

In the 1885 *A Memoir of The Late William Hodge, Sen.*, William Hodge Jr. also describes the burning. "All the remaining buildings, except Mrs. St. John's dwelling, the stone jail walls, a barnframe, and a blacksmith's shop, were destroyed. . . ." Regardless of whether the actual number standing was two or four, this means that over 100 buildings were destroyed. One count was that there were 66 wooden houses, 2 brick houses, 1 stone house, 16 stores, 35 barns, and 15 shops destroyed, with a total loss of $190,000.

And as devastating as the structural losses were, the human loss was more so. Soldiers were killed, scalped, their bodies left to freeze in the position of their death throes. There were the civilian losses such as Mrs. Lovejoy, too, whose dead body had been laid in her home at the end of the first attack, only to go up in flames with her house in the second.

Corroborating that Reese's blacksmith shop was saved, an account of the time says that it was in Reese's shop that the rest of dead were laid prior to burial. In all, during the two-day siege, 30 people were killed and 40 were wounded. Another 69 were captured and sent primarily to Montreal.

It is important to note at this point that although most histories, this one included, describe attacks on the Americans by Indians, these were Canadian Indians, aligned with the British. Many of the members of nations in the Iroquois Confederacy actually fought for America in this war. As Erastus Granger's grandson, in his brief biography of his grandfather, says, "As it was, the Nations remained neutral until . . . some of the Canadian Indians crossed the Niagara and invaded the Senecas' country, when at once the Nations sprang to arms and voluntarily joined the Americans."

REBUILDING INTO THE 1820s

Prior to the December attack by the British, the *Buffalo Gazette* had moved to the nearby Village of Williamsville. Throughout the next year the *Gazette* continued to publish accounts of the slow rebuilding efforts in Buffalo. Although some hardy souls returned within a week of the burning, the winter was hard that year and kept most people away in their makeshift homes. During the spring of 1814, settlers began to return to the village. They built new homes and commercial buildings.

By April 10, a military presence had been restored in the village, and these military operations helped increase settlement and trade. Troops remained in the village until late spring and the influx of money driven by the soldiers continued until they moved on to Canada in July.

With the arrival of fall came a successful battle across the lake in Fort Erie, thus ending the fighting in western New York well before the war ended. This battle, known as the Battle of Lundy's Lane, took place on July 25, 1814. While technically a draw, both sides in the battle fought well, sustained heavy casualties, and decided not to engage in further battles. It was a topic for lively discussion for decades in both Buffalo and Black Rock, and it made some of the area combatants local heroes. In December 1814, the Treaty of Ghent ended the war, although it was not officially signed until February the following year.

While some rebuilding took place in 1814, and many of the destroyed buildings had been replaced by July 1815, major redevelopment efforts did not start until well after the war ended. This was partly because the economy turned down again after the military left Buffalo in mid-1814. It was also because the citizens were waiting for aid from both New York State and the federal government for the damages they'd suffered. Reparations were a long way off, however, as the $80,000 that the federal government paid for the war's destruction did not arrive until 1825.

By then, the village had somewhat rebounded. The population in 1810 had been 1,508, but by 1820, it had grown by nearly 40 percent to 2,095. The growth rate decreased slightly in the next five years, with only 15 percent growth, raising the total to 2,412.

And the infrastructure to support the newcomers was also increasing, both in physical structures and services. By 1825, there were approximately 450 structures in the village. In addition to the public market on Stadnitski Avenue (Church Street), there were 36 grocery stores, 26 dry goods stores, and 8 warehouses. There were also seven clothing stores, six shoe stores, four drugstores, three hat stores, three jewelry stores, one hardware store, one looking glass store, eleven "houses of public entertainment," one rope walk, one brewery, one livery stable, one bank (Niagara), one custom house, one reading room, one insurance office, one post office, one public library, one masonic hall (but with two societies), and one theatre.

Among the building trades, there were 51 carpenters and 19 masons, as well as two cabinet making companies with a total of ten employees, three wheelwrights/ coach building businesses, also with ten employees, two chair makers with five employees, two painters with five employees, and one cooper with three employees. There were also numerous printing and metal-related service companies, including three printers with a total of ten employees, two book-binders with four employees, four goldsmiths with three employees, three tin and copper smiths employing a total of sixteen, and seven blacksmiths employing seventeen. The personal-related services employed the largest number of people with five boot and shoemakers employing 35, four tailors employing 20, three hatters with 8 employees, and one tobacconist with 2 employees. The professions included seventeen lawyers and nine doctors as well as four clergymen. Last, there were two tanning-related businesses, employing nine.

The one schoolhouse burned in 1813 had been replaced by four common schools, a private school for girls, and a private school for boys. There were four newspapers, all weekly, including *The Buffalo Patriot*, dating from 1811, *The Buffalo Journal* (1815), the *Gospel Advocate* (1823), and the *Buffalo Emporium* (1824). There were five religious congregations, one each of Baptist, Methodist, Episcopalian, Presbyterian, and Universalist.

Communication and transportation had also improved since the war. With only one bi-weekly mail delivery in 1803, by 1825 there were six mail routes with twenty weekly deliveries. There were nine daily stages and a steamship to Detroit.

BUILDING BUFFALO HARBOR

The economic situation had remained depressed until the mid-1820s, primarily because the village had no true harbor and hence no shipping commerce to attract businesses and settlers. Although Buffalo had been made a port of entry in 1805, most of the goods that arrived were shipped across Lake Ontario to the Niagara River, portaged around the Falls, then shipped again or sometimes carted to Black Rock, about 3 miles to Buffalo's north. Goods continuing west were loaded on ships that were then towed by oxen from Black Rock up the Niagara River to Lake Erie because the current was too strong to sail against. This added work made a direct port on Lake Erie desirable but not possible with Buffalo's existing physical layout.

Black Rock, on the other hand, had a great harbor and in 1818 the steamboat *Walk-in-the-Water* was built and launched there. This was the first steamboat on Lake Erie and was often referred to simply as "The Steamboat," as there were no others during its time. In fact, there were only 30 ships total on the lakes then.

Sailing between Black Rock and Detroit, the steamboat was a huge success. With fares ranging from $7 to $18, the 375-mile trip took less than two days. In its maiden voyage to Detroit, *Walk-in-the-Water* had 29 passengers. It arrived in Detroit in 44 hours and 10 minutes, which is an average of about 8.5 miles per hour. By its second voyage, ridership mushroomed to 120 people. According to one account, "the cabins of the *Walk-in-the-Water* were fitted up in a neat, convenient, and elegant style, and a trip to Buffalo was considered not only tolerable, but truly pleasant." The voyage continued to be popular until November 1821 when the boat was wrecked near Buffalo Creek. During that winter, a new boat named the *Superior* was commissioned and was the first to be built in Buffalo.

Even before the demise of the *Walk-in-the-Water*, Buffalo citizens realized that they needed two things to happen for ship commerce to increase. They needed a real harbor that could compete with Black Rock, and they needed some type of lighthouse. The need for a lighthouse was recognized in the early 1800s, and one was approved to be built in 1811, but this had to be postponed because of the War of 1812. In 1817, plans to build a lighthouse resurfaced, and Oliver Forward, who was the collector for the port of entry, purchased some land at the mouth of Buffalo Creek for $351.50. It is said that Forward paid for this land with his own funds.

By 1818, a 30-foot conical stone lighthouse was standing at the mouth of the creek. Unfortunately, the placement of the lighthouse and its proximity to the village often kept it hidden by the smoke the village produced. As Sheldon Ball put it:

> The light house is built of stone, and situated on a low sandy point, near the confluence of the waters of Buffalo Creek and Lake Erie. The light is elevated about thirty feet above the ordinary Lake level, but is of no great use to mariners, in consequence of the smoke and mists of the village, settling along the margin of the waters, just about the elevation of the lantern, which almost totally obscures the light; except when so near as to see it beneath, or at so great a distance, that it may be seen over the vapor. . . . This evil requires a remedy.

The lighthouse situation, coupled with the fact that there still was no real Buffalo harbor, kept the citizens aiming for major improvements. An early snow on October 24, 1819 caused problems for boats entering and leaving the harbor and further prompted the residents to get started on a harbor improvement project.

BUFFALO

This project began in 1820, with $1,861.25 in funds raised from the local citizens and a $12,000 loan from New York State. The original intent was to remove the sand bar that always blocked the mouth of the creek, but there was also a problem with the depth of the channel, too. So much so that the people building the *Superior* were concerned that it might not be able to launch on schedule because of it. But after 221 days of work, and a little luck from high water caused by a storm, the project was completed and the water was deep enough for the *Superior* and subsequent boats to navigate the new channel.

This relatively small change triggered an economic boom of unimagined strength, engulfing the city and its surrounding areas within a mere five years.

Chapter Four

ERIE CANAL DAYS

The planning for and building of the Erie Canal set the stage for Buffalo's tremendous growth throughout the nineteenth century. The Erie Canal was the largest civil engineering work in the United States at that time. When the city was incorporated in 1832, the population was approximately 10,000, nearly quadruple the population of 1825 when the canal opened. Following the fight with neighboring Black Rock over the canal terminus, the city experienced new growth into the 1850s.

SETTING THE STAGE

From the late 1700s until 1806, getting supplies and messages into western New York was tedious. Goods were transported from Albany in small boats, commonly referred to as Schenectady boats, west on the Mohawk River to Wood Creek, then in to Oneida Lake, to the Oswego River, and along the south shore of Lake Ontario to Lewiston or Queenston. Along the way boats needed to portage at several places. The trip took over a week. Then the goods needed to be transported in wagons down to Buffalo, with a load and capacity of 1 ton moving 12 miles per day or 18 miles per day on good roads.

As early as 1724, people started discussing the possibility of an inland canal route based on the canals in the Netherlands. In 1768, the colonial governor of New York, Sir Henry Moore, called for waterway improvements and between 1784 and 1792 several modifications to the natural waterways were authorized and made. By 1800, statesman Governeur Morris was suggesting a totally new canal be built, and in 1808 congress authorized a survey of potential routes.

The original commissioners appointed to study an inland canal in March of 1810 included Governeur Morris, Stephen Van Rensselear, Dewitt Clinton, Simeon DeWitt, William North, Thomas Eddy, and Peter Buell Porter. This commission was to present a feasibility report, which confirmed that the idea was doable. In April 1816, commissioners were changed to Stephen Van Rensselear, Dewitt Clinton, Samuel Young, Joseph Ellicott, and Myron Holley. This change in commissioners proved to be a turning point for the fledgling Buffalo because Ellicott, as a major Buffalo landholder, strongly advocated a canal route through Buffalo.

Another of the commissioners, and a major proponent of the canal, was then New York City Mayor Dewitt Clinton. As early as 1816, Clinton went on record as favoring the route end in Buffalo. Born in 1769, Clinton attended Columbia and studied law. He was the nephew of New York Governor George Clinton and followed his uncle into politics, serving in both the state senate and assembly and then in the U.S. Senate. In 1803, Clinton became mayor of New York City and also served in the New York Senate. He was elected lieutenant governor in 1811, while continuing to be mayor. Clinton was elected governor of New York in 1817, reelected in 1820, and again in 1824. He died in office in 1828, but not until after pushing through his pet project, forever maligned by his detractors as "Clinton's Ditch."

Despite the fact that many people thought the canal idea was a folly, the canal was given the go ahead, and work started in Rome on July 4, 1817. During his opening speech, commissioner Young said, "By this great highway, unborn millions will easily transport their surplus products to the shores of the Atlantic, procure their supplies, and hold a useful and profitable intercourse with all the maritime nations of the earth." Young's speech turned out to be prophetic.

The work on the canal was arduous, but laborers were relatively well compensated, earning from 80¢ to $1.87 per day for 10–14 hours of work. While this sounds low to us, this was roughly three times the going day rate in the early 1800s. For this wage, workers had to excavate the canal with mere pick-axes and shovels throughout much of the 363-mile route.

This central path through the state was largely forest at the time, so the workers also had to fell trees and pull the stumps. To do this, they invented a way to use leverage to make the work easier. They attached chains high up on a tree, then attached the other ends to a mule that pulled on the chains. Not only did the trees fall, but most of the roots came out of the ground, too. On average, it took five-and-a-half days for laborers working in teams of three to build three rods (about 45 feet) of canal bed, which was 40 feet wide at the top, 28 feet wide at the bottom, and 4 feet deep.

BATTLE WITH BLACK ROCK

Although work started on the central part of the canal in 1817, for the next five years the decision on the western terminus remained open. Peter Porter, who had led troops so valiantly in the War of 1812, owned businesses and resided in Black Rock and thus became the village's chief spokesperson.

Peter Buell Porter was born in 1773, graduated from Yale, and moved to western New York to practice law. Porter joined the militia and as a lieutenant colonel in 1807 helped lead the area in preparing for defense against possible aggression. In 1808, he was elected to the U.S. House of Representatives, and with his additional visibility, he was able to get a government customs house moved from Buffalo to Black Rock, where his portage business of Porter, Barton and Company was located.

When war broke out in 1812, Porter was appointed quartermaster general of the New York Militia, charged with leading about 13,000 men to defend the New York border all the way from Lake Erie to Lake Champlain. He was then made brigadier general of all western New York. In July 1813, the British invaded Black Rock and Porter retaliated by raiding and destroying the British encampment across the Niagara River. He was not in town in the winter of 1813 when the American troops again attacked Canada, nor when the British responded by burning Lewiston, Black Rock, and Buffalo. He did return to help fight the battle of Lundy's Lane and was considered the preeminent local hero.

Porter's local prominence continued with his involvement as a canal commissioner and helped fuel the fight between himself and Ellicott, and hence between Black Rock and Buffalo. Porter actually moved to Niagara Falls when Black Rock lost the canal terminus, and he lived there until 1844, when he died at age 74.

Although Porter eventually lost the canal battle, he was right to have put up the fight. The major advantage giving Black Rock an edge over Buffalo as the ultimate terminus of the Erie Canal was its harbor. Black Rock had a clear harbor entering into the Niagara River, but Buffalo's harbor was often blocked by a sandbar. This sandbar was noted by explorers as far back as the late 1600s and in several accounts of the War of 1812.

An address to the Buffalo Historical Society explained the problem like this:

> Buffalo Creek was navigable for canoes for some eight or ten miles above its mouth; in the lower part of its course for a mile or more it was deep enough to float the largest lake ship of the time, but there was a troublesome sandbar at its mouth and the entrance to the creek was uncertain, crooked and bad, making the inner harbor very difficult, and sometimes impossible, of entrance.

To say the least. This was no small sandbar. According to William Hodge, "the obstructing bar of sand was twenty rods wide, rising seven feet above the lake, and

BUFFALO

sixty rods long." That translates to approximately 330 feet wide and 990 feet long, no small obstruction.

Despite the huge disadvantage, Buffalo's advantage was that it sat on higher ground and directly on Lake Erie rather than the river. In 1818, a law was passed allowing the investigation of the redevelopment of the harbor in Buffalo. To help resolve the navigation and docking problem in Buffalo's harbor, the villagers decided to move the mouth of Buffalo Creek 60 rods (about 1,000 feet) further south by building two piers to keep the sandbar from clogging the creek. In his *History of Buffalo Harbor*, Thomas Symons described the harbor and these piers: "It consisted of a south pier composed of timber cribs filled with stone and brush, extending a quarter of a mile into the lake to 13 feet of water, and a north pier composed of a double row of piles filled with brush and stone. This north pier was about 1000 feet in length." Creating these piers and thus moving the harbor entrance, paid for by the $12,000 loan from New York State as well as private funds, eliminated the sandbar problem and won Buffalo the much sought after terminus spot.

In early 1822, Peter Porter and other influential Black Rock residents proposed construction of a pier in their harbor, and the canal commissioners agreed that if the pier project was successful, Black Rock would be named the winner. However, in the summer of 1822 at a meeting in Buffalo, the commission selected Buffalo as the western terminus of the canal. The meeting was held at the Eagle Tavern, owned by Benjamin Rathbun and located on Main near Court. Samuel Wilkeson was the spokesman for the Buffalo contingent and used his vast knowledge of the lake and navigation to present a convincing argument for Buffalo. This decision was almost reversed in 1823 when the Black Rock pier project proved successful, but it was not, largely because of the greater success of Buffalo's harbor project.

Since it can be said that Buffalo owes its existence to the improved harbor, it is not surprising that the driving force behind the harbor project, Samuel Wilkeson, is often credited with building the city. His gravestone in the Forest Lawn Cemetery proudly proclaims "Urbem Condidit," roughly meaning "he founded (built) this city." Born in Carlisle, Pennsylvania in 1781, Wilkeson was a sailor and ship owner who first visited the western New York area in 1812 when he was asked to help defend the border from British invasion with his ships. Although the village was later burned, Wilkeson was intrigued by the possibilities of the area and moved his family here in 1814. He brought with him enough materials to build a store and a house. He built the general store on the corner of Niagara and Main Streets and the house on the west side of Main south of Genesee. In 1815, he opened a meat market.

Wilkeson was appointed Buffalo's first justice of the peace in 1815, and he served as a village trustee from 1816 to 1817 and again from 1819 to 1821. As justice of the peace, "he smote the rascals and ruffians brought before him with terrible quickness and the utmost reach of the law." His largest contribution, however, starts in 1819 with his forming of the Buffalo Harbor Company. Along with his co-founders Ebenezer Walden, Ebenezer Johnson, Charles Townsend, George Coit, and Oliver Forward, the company was given a $12,000, 12-year loan from New York State to improve the Buffalo Harbor.

In 1820, with the company at risk of defaulting on the loan, Townsend, Forward, and Wilkeson pledged $8,000 each from personal finances to back the loan. Lest he lose his money, Wilkeson then took on the role of project manager for the harbor project. When workers attempted to quit because of the stormy and cold work conditions, Wilkeson, Townsend, and Forward installed temporary bulkheads by themselves. They then offered bonuses of $2 per month to compensate for working in the rain. The workers returned and completed the construction in 221 days, working from dawn to dusk, six days a week, with one half hour break for breakfast, one hour for dinner, and Sundays off.

With the harbor complete, Wilkeson continued to be a prominent citizen. He went on to be the first Erie County Court judge in 1821, a New York State assemblyman in 1822, and New York State senator in 1824. In the 1820s he built a new, grand Federal-style home on Niagara Square. In *Some Early Buffalo Characters*, Hollister commented, "The homestead, built by Judge Wilkeson in 1825, still stands on Niagara Square, a dignified monument in a way, to its builder who 'built the city.' " Unfortunately, this is no longer true. Wilkeson's home was torn down in 1915 and is now the site of City Hall, which is quite fitting.

His company, Wilkeson, Beals & Company, was the first to build a steam boiler in 1829 and he followed this up in 1845 by building the first smelting furnace to use raw bituminous coal. Despite his fervor for the canal, in 1831 Wilkeson was selected to serve on a committee to bring steam railroads from Albany to Buffalo. He was mayor in 1836, through one of the worst depressions in the city's history. He was 67 when he died in 1848.

PROSPERITY BECKONS

The Erie Canal, still considered one of the greatest engineering marvels of the modern world, opened with great fanfare on October 26, 1825. It had taken eight years, $7,143,000, and around 9,000 workers to build, and the state and municipalities along its route had planned a huge birthday party. In Buffalo, a grand parade through town ended with the boarding of the *Seneca Chief* by Governor Clinton and selected other dignitaries, including Samuel Wilkeson. As the boat left the harbor, cannon were fired, setting off a series of cannon fire all along the route to New York City. In this way, within two hours of the departure, New York City knew the *Seneca Chief* was en route.

The journey itself took considerably longer, primarily because the boat stopped frequently along the way to help local villages celebrate. It was nine days before the *Seneca Chief* arrived in New York City, and again, it was met with great excitement. On board, Clinton had stored two barrels of Lake Erie water, and in the much celebrated "Wedding of the Waters," he poured the water into the Atlantic. Thus began an era of untold prosperity for New York City, Buffalo, and most of the towns along the way.

Running from Albany to Buffalo, through Utica, Syracuse, Rochester, and dozens of small towns, the original canal was a total of 363 miles. It used 84 locks to negotiate the 564-foot rise and each lock was 90 feet long and 12 feet wide. The canal itself was 40 feet wide at the top, 28 feet wide at the bottom, and 4 feet deep. Numerous aqueducts and one culvert helped the canal cross creeks and roads, and hundreds of "low bridges" also crossed the canal.

Freight boats on the canal could travel at 36–55 miles per day, carry up to 30 tons, and had a 2.5 foot draft. In 1825, the first year it was completed for the entire route, 13,100 boats paid $500,000 in tolls. And the shippers reveled at the savings. On the overland route to New York City, shipping 1 ton of flour worth $40 took three to six weeks at a cost of $100–$120. On the canal, the same amount of flour on boats drawn by two mules could make the trip in eight or nine days at a cost of $6 per ton. By 1829, the canal traffic shipped 3,640 bushels of wheat; by 1837, 500,000 bushels, and by 1841, 1 million bushels.

Passenger traffic could travel at 100 miles per day. This means it took travelers only four days to get from New York City to Buffalo, a vast improvement over the old trip duration of a week or more. Several of these early canal travelers chronicled their trips along the way and also noted what they found in Buffalo. In 1829, an anonymous visitor tells us, "At Buffalo, which supports six extensive Hotels, a Theatre and three Churches, the grand Canal terminates by another spacious Basin, filled with boats."

While this account is benign, Frances Trollope, in an 1828 visit, was much less kind:

> Of all the thousand and one towns I saw in America I think Buffalo is the
> queerer looking; it is not quite so wild as Lockport, but all the buildings

have the appearance of having been run up in a hurry, though every thing has, an air of great pretension; there are porticoes, columns, domes, and colonnades, but all in wood. Every body tells you there . . . that their improvement and their progression are more rapid, more wonderful, than the earth ever before witnessed; while, to me, the only wonder is how so many thousands, nay millions of persons, can be found, in the nineteenth century, who can be content so to live.

She then goes on to describe her hotel and some of the bill of fare:

The Eagle Hotel, an immense wooden fabric, has all the pretension of a splendid establishment; but its monstrous corridors, low ceilings, and intricate chambers, gave me the feeling of a catacomb rather than a house. We arrived after the table d'hote teadrinking was over, and supped comfortably enough . . .; but the next morning we breakfasted in a long, low, narrow room, with a hundred persons, and anything less like comfort can hardly be imagined.

Trollope also complains about the natural surroundings: "Lake Erie has no beauty to my eyes; it is not the sea, and it is not the river, nor has it the beautiful scenery generally found round smaller lakes. The only interest its unmeaning expanse gave me arose from remembering that its waters, there so tame and tranquil, were defined to leap the gulf of Niagara."

Despite these less than stellar words of recommendation, the canal was a huge success. The harbor bustled with activity. In 1820, prior to the opening of the improved harbor, 120 ships docked. By 1825 it jumped to 359, and by 1827 it had nearly tripled to 972. By 1844, upwards of 300 boats could dock simultaneously.

The tolls paid for the entire project within nine years, and perhaps more importantly, the canal enabled the development of not just Buffalo, but all the towns along the way. Subsequent railroad and highway development paralleled the canal to such an extent that still today, 80 percent of New York's population lives within 25 miles of the canal or the Hudson River.

OFFICIALLY A CITY

With Francis Trollope's account an exception, most travelers to the area touted the benefits of Buffalo, which, in turn, encouraged more people to travel here.

BUFFALO

And thousands of them stayed. Although several of the prominent citizens were concerned about how much development might take place with Ellicott still owning or controlling the "prime" parcels, by 1831, the village had grown large enough to petition to become a city. The population at that time was approximately 10,000, nearly quadruple the population of 1825 when the canal opened.

In 1832, the City of Buffalo was chartered by New York State to include an area of approximately 4.5 square miles. Several pieces of the original city charter shed great light on the progressive attitudes of the early city officials and residents. Most striking was that both black and white men were given the right to vote directly in the charter. This was extremely early in American urban history for such rights. Also progressive at the time was that the city officials could regulate the location of slaughterhouses, as well as building heights, materials, and chimneys to avoid fire.

Only inn-keepers could sell alcohol (or give it away) for consumption on their premises and they had to be licensed to do so. Property owners were required to build and maintain their own sidewalks or the City would do so and charge the owners. The City also required written sales records of the transfer of all properties and legal notices to be placed in public papers. It was allowed to regulate all the public highways as well as the waters of Big Buffalo Creek and Little Buffalo Creek.

The charter created a Board of Health allowed to inspect boats docking in the harbor and refuse them entry if sickness or disease warranted. Unfortunately, this portion of the charter came in handy in the next few months when a cholera epidemic broke out.

Some of the more humorous regulations included interdictions on flying kites, rolling hoops, or playing ball on public streets or sidewalks, and playing cards, dice, or similar games in stores even if no betting was taking place. No billiards nor bowling was allowed and the city could regulate the "quality of bread."

The charter was approved in April and the Common Council members were elected on May 26. In the original charter, the Common Council appointed the mayor, so at the first council meeting two days later, the members appointed Dr. Ebenezer Johnson to the seat. He served a second term in office during the 1834–1835 election year.

Johnson was born in New England in November 1786 but studied medicine with Dr. White in Cherry Valley, New York. In 1809, he headed to Buffalo to open a medical office and drugstore. Unfortunately for Johnson, Cyrenius Chapin had beat him to that. Lacking funds and deciding that the small settlement was not ready for two doctors or two drugstores, he worked at odd jobs. When the War of

1812 erupted, Johnson accepted a position as an assistant surgeon and kept it until the end of the war. Because of this, he was not in town with his family when the village was burned.

Following the war, rather than attempt to continue practicing medicine, Johnson opened a business with Samuel Wilkeson. He also started purchasing real estate. In 1814, he bought lot 63 on Main Street and lot 30 on Delaware. He later bought the entire block of about 25 acres on Delaware between Chippewa and Tupper and west to the reservation. On the Main Street lot, he built a frame house, living there until he built another house, this one of stone on Delaware. The latter house would be used for the Buffalo Female Academy in later years. Some of this land is now the site of Johnson Park, named after him. As an early profile noted:

> He was an exceedingly prompt and energetic business man, distinguished
> for his punctuality and industry, and was, until the reverses of 1836, one
> of the wealthiest citizens in Western New York. . . . It is no disparagement
> of many excellent officers who have administered the affairs of the city to
> say that a more active and efficient chief magistrate never presided over the
> Corporation of Buffalo.

By the time of its incorporation, Buffalo had six churches, including a Protestant Episcopal, a Baptist, a Methodist Episcopal, and a Universalist. There were also two banks and an insurance company. Instead of the original Indian trading posts and taverns, there were ten general stores. A library had been established and had an inventory of 700 books. The school system that started with the one room schoolhouse in 1808 consisted of ten schools, both public and private.

The same year as the incorporation, a terrible cholera epidemic hit the city. It started in Montreal, Canada with 3,000 deaths in 11 days, then spread south down the Champlain Canal to Albany. From there it continued on down the Hudson River to New York City and west toward Buffalo. It also approached Buffalo down the St. Lawrence to Toronto and across Lakes Ontario and Erie. That year, 120 people died from the disease.

Cholera is a bacterial infection of the intestine usually spread through contaminated water, but in the 1800s, no one knew what caused the disease, how it spread, or how to cure it. Symptoms started out inauspiciously enough with diarrhea and vomiting, then severe spasms. As short as a few hours after the first symptoms, those afflicted would go into a dehydration-induced shock and die. People who could replenish fluids quickly enough usually survived.

City aldermen organized a board of health in June of 1832, and after the death of an Irish laborer on July 16 and another death the next day, the board of health opened a temporary hospital in the brick McHose House building on Niagara. This building had been originally built on speculation as a tavern for the canal, but was vacant at the time.

To try to stem the disease, steamboats were stopped at the harbor entrance and passengers inspected. Stagecoaches were halted on the roads outside the city and canal boats just below Black Rock. Still, the disease spread, especially to several of the attendants in the hospital who caught it and died. As Lewis Allen described in his address to the Buffalo Historical Society, "The disease darted like forked lightning at right angles, at obtuse angles, at oblique angles, up one street, down another alley, and into any and almost every quarter of the little city." Tales abounded of men working all day, going home, and being dead by 9:00 p.m.

The disease returned again in 1834, worse than before, taking former mayor Major A. Andrews. It returned periodically over the following decades and was especially bad again in 1849 and 1854. The 1849 recurrence reported 3,000 cases with more than 900 dead.

In 1844, tragedy of a different type hit the city. On October 18, a storm caused the lake to rise 2 feet. This massive rush of water wiped out one third of the stone pier, damaged the central wharf area, and completely flooded the lowland areas east of Main and south of Seneca. It also took down several homes, the engine house of the Buffalo and Attica Railroad, and the H. Hodge and Company glass factory. In all, 30–40 people drowned.

First Wave Immigrants

Buffalo through the early 1900s was largely a city of immigrants, and the first to arrive en masse were the Irish. Most of the first wave of Irish came during the building of the Erie Canal, and then stayed, although some records suggest that as early as 1815, an Irishman named Patrick O'Rourke had settled here.

While a good sized group of an estimated 400 Irish were here by the incorporation in 1832, the major influx occurred in the 1840s as a result of the potato famine in Ireland. Nearly 2 million Irish immigrated to the United States between 1840 and 1860, and most of them chose to settle in port areas such as Buffalo. It is thought that around 90 percent of the 900-some dead in the 1849 outbreak of cholera were Irish because they lived in the poorest section of the city at that time. By the 1870 census, there were over 10,000 Irish immigrants living in the city.

Until the late 1800s, many of these Irish immigrants worked on the docks as scoopers, shoveling the grain off arriving ships into storage bins that were later scooped back into departing ships. This was grueling, back-breaking work and seasonal. Many of the scoopers had part-time jobs in other trades to help make ends meet.

Perhaps the most influential Irishman to arrive in Buffalo was the first bishop of the Buffalo Catholic Diocese, Bishop John Timon. Appointed to his position in 1847, Timon's influence is still seen in many of today's communities. The Buffalo Diocese was created in April 1847 and at that time encompassed 20 western New York counties. Although this sounds like a large responsibility, Timon's diocese originally included only 16 Catholic churches.

Born in Pennsylvania in 1797, Timon was ordained in 1825 in St. Louis and spent the next 22 years as a missionary along the Mississippi River and later in Texas. Although he turned down the position of Perfect Apostolic offered him in Texas in 1840, preferring his clerical role, he did accept bishop of the Buffalo diocese. When the new Buffalo diocese was formed in 1847, he was pleased to accept the bishopship, arriving here in October that same year.

In his 20 years in the city, Timon helped set up several institutions, largely by bringing a variety of different Catholic orders to town. These included the Jesuits, the Vincentians, the Franciscans, the Sisters of Charity, the Ladies of the Sacred Heart, and the Sisters of St. Frances. The Sisters of Charity was one of the first groups to heed his call, arriving in 1848. Some of the institutions created in his tenure are St. Joseph's orphanage (1851), the Foundling home (1853), St. Mary's School for the Deaf (1853), and numerous schools, colleges, convents, and seminaries. Timon died in 1867 and is buried in St. Joseph's Cathedral.

Germans also immigrated to the area before there was a city. Credited as the first German in Buffalo is John Kucherer, who moved here from Pennsylvania in 1821. Kucherer is often called "Water John" because he sold lake water door to door from his cart. The next German in town was Jakob Siebold, who arrived in 1822 from Wurttemberg. Siebold ran a grocery store on the west side of Main Street and helped found Buffalo Savings Bank and the Buffalo Chamber of Commerce. He was 71 when he died in 1863.

Another key German immigrant was Rudolph Baer, who moved into town in 1826. Baer is distinctive because in 1827, on the corner of Main and Ferry, he brewed the first beer in the original city limits. Following in Baer's footsteps, in 1833, Moffat and Service, at Mohawk and Morgan, became the first brewery in the city. In 1876, Service took over the business. By 1884, there were 19 breweries and 14 malt houses in the city. At their peak in the late 1800s, there were more than three dozen breweries in the city; one of the largest number in the country.

While some Germans may have arrived here in the early 1820s, the first major influx was in 1828, when a group of farmers settled on what was known then as "the Buffalo Plains." Immigration continued throughout the first half of the century, reaching its peak between 1848 and 1849. By 1850, there were 42,000 Germans in the city. As Orasmus Turner noted in his 1850 book on the Holland Purchase, "The location of German emigrants upon the Holland Purchase, forms a prominent feature of recent events. In Buffalo, they already compose nearly one-third of the entire population, and are mingled in almost all its branches of business."

Although many of the early Irish immigrants had been day laborers, the German immigrants were primarily tradesmen, who according to one account were "industrious, unassuming and frugal with materials they procured for themselves." Many were also public officials, following in the footsteps of the first German public official, Philip Dorsheimer (sometimes spelled Dorschheimer or Dorscheimer). Dorsheimer moved to the United States in 1815 or 1816, coming first to Pennsylvania and then living for 11 years in Lyons, New York, also an Erie Canal town. He started out as a miller there but soon took over running a variety of hotels. From the travelers lodging with him, presumably, he heard about the wonders of Buffalo, for he and his wife and young son William moved to town in 1836.

Upon arriving, Dorsheimer ran the Farmer's Hotel at Main Street near Seneca. Later he took over at the Mansion House and turned it into a rather famous city spot. In 1838 he was appointed postmaster and continued in that job through 1847. He went on to be elected New York State's treasurer in 1859, serving until 1861, and was then customs inspector under Lincoln's presidency. Dorsheimer is said to have been an interpreter for the Ebenezer Inspirationalists when they purchased their land in West Seneca in 1842–1843. One humorous biographer noted, "He knew how to convince the most respected Americans that he was the most influential German, not only in Buffalo but of the entire United States." Dorsheimer died in 1868. He was 71.

INDUSTRY AND INVENTION

From just one steamboat and 30 total craft on the lake in 1818, with the opening of the canal, ship traffic had increased dramatically. By 1843, there were approximately 60 steamboats operating and about 300 schooners and other sailboats. Many of these boats were passenger vessels, running to and from several mid-western cities. For an average fare of $12, Buffalonians and other travelers could take the 1,047 mile trip to Chicago every other day. For $7, they could go daily to Detroit.

In 1826, the federal government had taken over maintenance of the Buffalo harbor, and it continued to make improvements. The government constructed a more substantial pier, and at the end, in 1832–1833, built the current limestone lighthouse. The lighthouse is octagonal in shape, 20 feet in diameter at the base tapering to 12 feet in diameter at the top, 50 feet high to the base of the light, and 75 feet high total.

The ingenuity used in transforming Buffalo's harbor continued to be a city hallmark throughout the nineteenth century. The most critical invention for both the city and the grain shipping industry occurred in 1841, when Joseph Dart created the first steam-powered grain elevator. By that year, Buffalo's harbor was receiving nearly 2 million bushels of grain and the work crews just couldn't unload them fast enough. Bulk grain was unloaded from a boat in baskets, then weighed, then carried into a warehouse. This tedious method of unloading and storing meant that at most 2,000 bushels per day could be handled. In rainy or windy weather, nothing could be unloaded, and these weather conditions occurred on average once every four days.

Building on a device invented by Oliver Evans for use in milling, Dart was convinced there was a better way. "I believed, however, that I could build a warehouse, of large capacity for storage, with an adjustable Elevator and Conveyors, to be worked by steam; and so arranged as to transfer grain from vessels to boats or bins, with cheapness and dispatch." Despite claims that he was mad and the scheme would never work, in the fall of 1842, Dart began building his warehouse. And luckily for Buffalo, it worked wonderfully.

With 2-quart buckets placed on the conveyor 28 inches apart, Dart's first elevator could unload 1,000 bushels per hour. To put this into perspective, that was 50 percent of the maximum amount the traditional method could unload in a full day. This cut time in port immensely, as shown in this story: A ship from Ohio carrying 4,000 bushels of wheat came in and unloaded, returned home, came back, and unloaded a second time before the ships that docked with her on her original arrival could be unloaded. Dart's elevator was so successful, he had to turn down requests for unloading and storage because his elevator was often full. His first elevator could hold only 55,000 bushels, but in 1845, he expanded it to 110,000 bushels.

Not content with the status quo in speed either, Dart continued to improve the conveyor mechanism. He moved the buckets closer together, first to 22 inches, then 16, and was able to double his speed to 2,000 bushels an hour; the equivalent of one day's work manually. Later elevators used 8-quart buckets spaced 12 inches apart, capable of raising 7,000 bushels an hour.

BUFFALO

While Dart was improving the grain shipping and storing industry, changes were also developing with another largely steam-powered application known as railroads. By 1842, there were four ways to get to Buffalo from Albany; by land, by canal, by a combination of steamboats, land and other boats, and by the newly opened rail lines. The canal had been the fastest route, however, until the railroads surpassed it. They were faster for two reasons: they traveled at a greater speed and they traveled a shorter distance. The canal route to Buffalo was 363 miles, while the rail route was 325. The shortest distance was by road, only 284 miles, but the roads then were still poorly developed.

To get to Buffalo from Albany, train travelers would take a series of small lines to Rochester. From Rochester, they would use the Tonawanda Railroad through Bergen, then Batavia and on to Attica, where the line ended. From Attica, a line named the Attica and Buffalo Railroad traveled the remaining 31 miles into Buffalo.

There was also a short line called the Buffalo and Black Rock Railroad, which ran a mere 3 miles, as well as the Buffalo and Niagara Falls Railroad, 23 miles long, running between the respective areas. The Buffalo and Black Road railroad cost $7,500 to build; however, it used horse-drawn cars. Connecting to the Lockport and Niagara Railroad, the Buffalo and Niagara Falls Railroad was incorporated in 1834 and cost $110,000.

While the railroads combined with the canal to make Buffalo an attractive place for conducting business, other amenities were inducing people to establish residencies. In an 1842 travel guide, John Disturnell was especially proud of Buffalo's roads and the buildings. "The streets in the most compact portions of the city, are paved and the buildings, particularly those for business, are of the most durable construction, and modern style."

Disturnell also noted the types of establishments in the city at that time. Under municipal buildings and offices were a county court house, clerk's office, and jail, as well as city offices. The latter were located on the second floor of one of the two public markets. In addition to these markets, there were 13 forwarding houses, and several other stores. Public-oriented businesses included a theater, an insurance company, several hotels/taverns, mechanics, and two banks.

Other services included two silver platers, eight print shops, two book publishers, two book binders, and two chemical laboratories. There were also one each of the following types of factories: steam engine, steam planing, Britannia ware, blanket, lead pipe, starch, saleratus, and morocco. There were three carriage factories, five soap and candle factories, two lock factories, and four tobacco factories, but the highest business concentration by far was the fourteen breweries. The mills, tanneries, and foundries included a flour mill, a sawmill, a Burr millstone, and two tanneries, as well as one type and stereotype foundry, two iron, and two brass foundries. Rounding out the list, there was a federally-run brick barracks, a shipyard, and an orphan asylum.

In addition to the train and ship travel lines noted earlier, travelers to and from Buffalo could also take daily stages west to Detroit, with stops in Erie, Cleveland, and Toledo, for $10 and east to Batavia for $1. When the canal was closed for the winter, a daily stage also ran to Lockport for $1.50 per person. Three times per week, there were stages to Ellicottville ($2.50) and Warsaw ($1.50).

Industry and invention can have negative impacts, too, and one of the most devastating during this time was perpetrated by Benjamin Rathbun. Rathbun had moved to Buffalo in the 1820s and by 1825 was operating the Eagle Tavern, one of the primary meeting places in town. By the mid-1830s Rathbun was a, if not the, leading citizen of Buffalo. In addition to various stagecoach lines, he owned construction companies, stone quarries, brick factories, and other building-related enterprises. But in 1836, the bottom fell out of Rathbun's businesses when it was found that his brother and nephew had been forging the signature's of several leading citizens to get loans. Despite the fact that Rathbun was not directly involved in the scheme and that his brother and nephew had skipped town, he was convicted of fraud and sentenced to five years in jail. The collapse of his empire started a depression in Buffalo and the surrounding areas that purportedly led to the nationwide depression of 1837. A remaining legacy from this time is his 1833 Title Guarantee Building, formerly the First Unitarian Church. This building is said to be the oldest in downtown Buffalo on its original site.

COMMUNITY INSTITUTIONS GROW

Despite the panic of 1837, the constant influx of people into Buffalo required more building. Homes, churches, commercial enterprises, and streets all sprang up at nearly record speeds. By 1836, one street had 1,000 feet of paving. There were sewers on three streets totaling about a mile of pipes. There were four omnibuses, which ran hourly up Main Street and once in a while to Black Rock. There was even one fledgling horse-draw railroad.

Yet in the 25 years from the opening of the canal through 1850, some of the most intensive building revolved around the religious affiliations of the new Buffalo citizens. Roman Catholic, Protestant, and Jewish immigrants came to the city in large enough quantities to require new or expanded churches. By 1850, these groups had established 17 churches in the following denominations: Lutheran (three),

Presbyterian (three), Roman Catholic (two), African (two), Episcopal (two), Unitarian, Universalist, Baptist, Jewish, and Methodist.

One of the earliest churches started on January 5, 1829, when Louis Stephan Le Couteulx, a French nobleman who had purchased a large tract of land in Buffalo in 1804, donated a parcel on Edward Street to Bishop Dubois, then bishop of New York. Le Couteulx had moved to Buffalo in 1803 and was a strong proponent of the Catholic Church, holding meetings in his house for a number of years. In addition to this first parcel of land, he would later donate the lots for another church, Immaculate Conception, two asylums, the Buffalo Orphan and Infant asylums, and the Deaf Mute Institute.

Three years later, in 1832, construction began on the first Catholic church, St. Louis Church. It was a small wooden structure and was soon outgrown by its congregation of Irish, French, and German immigrants. In 1837 the Irish formed a separate congregation. For two years they rented space over a store at Main and Terrace, then built a church on Broadway at Ellicott in 1839, which they called St. Patrick's. The French parishioners of St. Louis soon did the same thing, building a church on Clinton and Washington in 1846. This left the original St. Louis church with a primarily German congregation. Father Alexander Par was the pastor of St. Louis in 1835 when the wood structure was demolished and replaced with a new brick one.

In 1843, several of the parishioners who had left the St. Louis church and were worshiping in St. Patrick's on Broadway decided to build their own church. St. Mary's was completed in May of 1844 and closed again in 1848. A new St. Mary's opened in July of 1850.

Many Lutherans were also early settlers in Buffalo and they, too, built some wonderful churches, the first of which was St. John's Evangelical Lutheran Parish. Founded in 1828, this parish met for four years on the second story of a grocery store. In September 1832 work began on the church on Hickory Street.

During this era, the Jewish were also establishing temples. The first Jewish settler was a German language teacher named Flersheim who arrived in town somewhere around 1835. But since it took at that time ten men over the age of 13 to hold a service, it wasn't until 1847 that the first known Jewish service was held in a public venue, the Concert Hall at Main and Swan. Later that year, the Beth El congregation was formed. Worship services were held in the top floor of the Hoyt building at Main and Eagle (where Main Place Mall is today) for over two years. In 1850, Beth El bought the school on Pearl near Eagle and turned it into a synagogue. The Beth Zion congregation spun off from Beth El in 1850.

One of the most historic churches established during this era was the Michigan Avenue Baptist Church, still standing at 511 Michigan. An outgrowth of the first Baptist church in town, the Washington Street Baptist Church, this African-American congregation started its separate worship services sometime between 1827 and 1836 and was originally known as the Second Baptist Church. Since the time of Joseph Hodge, African Americans were settling in Buffalo. Although their major immigration would not occur until the twentieth century, by 1850 it is estimated that there were approximately 300 African Americans living in the city. Many of them lived in neighborhoods around Michigan and Broadway and the congregation thought having a church in that area would be good for the community.

They started raising funds for a separate facility in 1842, laid the cornerstone on the present church in 1845, and finished the building in 1849. During the next few decades, the church would be used as an Underground Railroad stop for escaped slaves fleeing to Canada. The congregation would go through hard times in the late 1800s and one of its patrons, Eric Hedstrom, regularly provided free coal and other supplies. Hedstrom was also instrumental in 1892 in bringing to Buffalo the church's pastor, J. Edward Nash, who then served for 61 years. Reverend Nash and one of his parishioners, Mary Talbert, were influential in organizing the Niagara Movement, the predecessor organization to the National Association for the Advancement of Colored People (NAACP). Other than a small addition and interior remodel in 1908, the church remains much as it was when originally built. It is listed on the National Register of Historic Places and a local preservation group is in the process of raising funds for a complete restoration.

While all of these churches were important to the development of the community, the most architecturally significant church building constructed during this time was St. Paul's Episcopal Cathedral. Located at Main and Church Streets, this structure was designed in 1849 by noted church architect Richard Upjohn in his typical Gothic style. Replacing the first permanent church in Buffalo, which had been built on this same site in 1819, the red Medina sandstone building has dominated its corner for over 150 years. The whole church was said to have cost around $100,000, and the 10-bell chimes reportedly cost $15,000. It was originally built without spires on its two towers, but once the 270-foot main spire/tower was completed in 1870, St. Paul's became the tallest building in the city, an honor it held for many years.

Though severely damaged in 1888 by one of the fires caused by too much gas pressure in the gas lines, the church continues to reflect much of Upjohn's original design. Now somewhat dwarfed by 1960s skyscrapers, this National Historic Landmark is still the best known religious structure in Buffalo.

BUFFALO

Another important contribution to the community during this time was not a church but a university. Founded in 1846, the University of Buffalo started simply enough with a medical school and has grown into one of the four major New York State university centers. Originally housed in a building at Washington and Seneca, in 1849 the medical school moved into a new building on the corner of Main and Virginia. The department continued to occupy this building until 1893.

Two asylums and a private hospital were also established prior to 1850. The first, the Buffalo Orphan Asylum, was organized in 1835. A building was built on Virginia Street in 1850 and held on average 80 patients. The second asylum was the Buffalo Female Orphan Asylum, which was founded in 1848. It was located on the corner of Broadway and Ellicott and had a capacity of around 100 children.

Also on Virginia Street was the Buffalo Hospital of the Sisters of Charity, which was founded in 1848. There were 20 hospital wards with a total capacity of around 150 patients.

And with this rapidly improving community infrastructure, its thriving port, and leading citizens such as Millard Fillmore, Philip Dorsheimer and his son William, and William Fargo, Buffalo was poised for greatness in the declining years of the nineteenth century.

Chapter Five

CIVIL WAR LOOMS AND PASSES

By 1855, Buffalo's population had mushroomed to nearly 75,000. Much of this growth was based on the business created by the Erie Canal and the infant railroad industry, especially in the lumber, coal, and grain trades. In 1855, Buffalo was the largest grain port in the world, and the total amount of goods shipped through Buffalo was valued at nearly $50 million at a time when average wages were $52 per year. And two American presidents hailed from Buffalo during the period from 1850 to 1890.

OUR CITY, OUR PRESIDENTS

The 1850 population of the city was 42,261, and by 1860 it had increased dramatically to 81,129, largely due to the revised city charter of 1853. When the city was chartered in 1832, it had five voting wards. The number of wards expanded to 13 in 1853, as the city increased its borders, annexing many of the smaller hamlets near the city core, including its one-time rival Black Rock. The revision of the city lines increased the north boundary from North Street to the Kenmore line, about 5 miles from city center. The east boundary moved from Jefferson to a line 4 miles east and the south boundary also to a line about 4 miles south. The west boundary stayed the same, ending at the river and lake shores.

This expansion made the city approximately 9 miles long and 3–5 miles wide. The total area of the new city grew ten-fold to 42 square miles. It increased the value of the city's real estate by more than $3 million and instantly added 30,000 people as city residents.

With the new charter, the local election day was moved to November to align with election day in national and state elections. In the original charter in 1832, the mayor was a member of the Common Council and was elected to one-year terms by the council. In the revised charter, though, the mayor was elected for two-year terms, by the public, and was no longer president of the Common Council. Many of the previously appointed positions also became elected ones, including recorder, superintendent of schools, chief of police, overseer of the poor, comptroller, treasurer, receiver of taxes, street commissioner, city attorney, and city surveyor. None of the elected officials could serve consecutive terms.

But political reorganization was not the only change in Buffalo. In the 25 years from 1836 to 1861, the 1,000 feet of paving on one street had grown into 52 miles of "superior" paving on 137 city streets. The sewer systems had also expanded. From 1 mile of pipes in 1836, by 1861, there were 52 miles of lines on 124 streets. According to Guy Salisbury in his speech about the improvements in the city, the sewer system alone provided "benefits of which to the public health, cleanliness and comfort will be incalculable."

Along with the new sewer system, there was public water, both to homes and, more importantly, to fire hydrants, which would help minimize fire damage. The city also had one of the most extensive gas lighting systems in the country, with 53 miles of pipes lighting 2,100 street lamps. These lamps, said Salisbury, "are in brilliant contrast with the sombre gloom through which we used to grope our way." The waterfront was also expanding. By 1861, there were 13 miles of developed frontage.

The four omnibuses that had run in 1836 had expanded to 60. There were 11 miles of "double-track street railways," with the cars running not hourly, but every five to ten minutes. The railroads had also matured. The one in 1836 had grown to more than five, including the Buffalo and State Line; Buffalo, New York and Erie; Buffalo and Lake Huron; New York Central; and New York and Erie.

This infrastructure growth paralleled the population growth. From the 1850s to the 1890s, immigration into the United States continued at record levels. More than 7 million people arrived from Europe and other areas to seek their version of the American Dream. As with the first wave of immigrants, many of these settled in Buffalo. By 1890, 35 percent of the Buffalo population was born abroad, ranking the city 11th in the nation in both total population and in the percentage of foreign-born residents. Although Germans and Irish were still moving here until the early 1860s, the larger migrations in the late 1800s were from the Italians and Polish.

Following Joseph Hodge's quest for freedom, African Americans continued to move here throughout the mid- to late 1800s. By 1855 there were approximately 700 African Americans living in Buffalo, coming primarily from the Southern states seeking freedom. In these early years, they lived throughout the city, not in specific areas as did the European immigrants.

Several years after the expansion of the city boundaries, it was obvious that the city and county government had outgrown the offices at Church and Franklin. In 1871, Franklin Square was selected as the best cite for a new structure. Five years later, in

1876, the new, three-story, approximately $2 million building was opened. Still used as County Hall, the central bell tower is more than 200 feet tall.

Also built during this time was Buffalo's famous Forest Lawn Cemetery, developed on 80 acres of land originally owned by Erastus Granger. Although the land was purchased in 1849, development didn't start until 1850, and it was later that same year that the first lots were purchased and people interred. In 1851, the bodies from the Franklin Square Cemetery were moved to Forest Lawn. Located between downtown and Delaware Park, the cemetery became a popular picnic and walking area over the next several decades. It continued to expand with various land purchases and is now 269 acres.

The city's infrastructure wasn't the only thing drawing attention and praise, though. During the four decades from 1850 through 1890, two Buffalo leaders would gain national acclaim. Both Millard Fillmore (1800–1874) and Grover Cleveland (1837–1908) hailed from Buffalo, going on to become American presidents. Millard Fillmore was born in rural New York State in 1800 and moved to Buffalo in 1820 to study law. In 1823, he was admitted to the Erie County Bar and then moved to East Aurora to set up a practice. He returned to Buffalo in 1830. He opened a law practice first with Joseph Clary and later with Nathan Hall and quickly became popular. Fillmore favored the new Anti-Masonic tenets and because of this was elected to the New York State Legislature in 1828. Four years later, he was sent to the U.S. Congress, also through the Anti-Masonic party. He transferred his allegiance to the Whig party in 1834, but Fillmore did not run for reelection that year, choosing instead to wait until 1836. He was reelected in 1836 as a Whig and stayed in office for the next six years.

Fillmore ran for governor of New York in 1844 but was defeated by Silas Wright. Disappointed, he accepted the job of state comptroller in 1847. In the meantime, he had several civic roles to keep him busy. In 1846, he was appointed the first chancellor of the newly established University of Buffalo and continued to serve in this role until he died.

Fillmore's political aspirations were finally fulfilled in 1848 when Zachary Taylor was nominated for president of the United States and Fillmore was nominated for vice-president. They won the election, but in 1850, Taylor died and Fillmore became President, serving out the remaining two years. Most political commentators say that Fillmore was a good but not great President, largely because of his policies on slavery and immigration. Although he didn't favor slavery, he also didn't favor abolishing it in the Southern states. In fact, he signed into law the Fugitive Slave Act, forcing northerners to return any runaway slaves they found. He was also concerned about the high number of immigrants coming to the United States. Both these opinions were unpopular with the Whigs and combined to lose him his party's nomination for reelection in 1852.

After his term was over, Fillmore returned to Buffalo, living first at 180 Franklin Street. He ran again for President in 1856 on the Know-Nothing ticket but did not fare well and decided to retire from politics. His wife died in 1853 from complications of a cold she caught at the inaugural address of Fillmore's successor, and his daughter died in the 1854 cholera outbreak, so he busied himself again with community commitments. In 1855, he was one of the founders of Buffalo General Hospital, and he helped found the Buffalo Historical Society in 1862. He served as the first president of the latter from 1862 to 1867, and that year, 1867, founded and was elected first president of the Buffalo Club. He also founded the local SPCA in 1873.

In 1858, Fillmore remarried, this time to a wealthy widow from Albany. That same year they moved into a mansion on Niagara Square. While residing there, such famous people as ex-President John Quincy Adams and future President Abraham Lincoln came to visit. Fillmore continued to live in Buffalo until his death in 1874. He is buried in Forest Lawn Cemetery with both wives, his mother-in-law, and children.

The second President to hail from Buffalo, Stephen Grover Cleveland, moved to the city from Holland Patent, New York in 1855, shortly after Fillmore retired. Born in New Jersey in 1837, Cleveland moved to Buffalo to work with his uncle, Lewis Allen, who lived in Black Rock. His uncle also arranged for him to clerk in a law office, where he studied dutifully and was admitted to the Bar in 1859, just before the outbreak of the Civil War. Cleveland was eligible for the draft during the war but in 1862, he paid $500 to a Polish immigrant to take his place. His tactic worked, leaving him to pursue his career, being elected that same year to supervisor of the second ward.

In 1863, Cleveland was appointed assistant district attorney for Erie County. Seven years later, Cleveland was elected Erie County sheriff and served in that role through 1873. Also in 1870, he was appointed to the board of the newly formed New York State Normal School (currently Buffalo State) which would open the following year. By 1882, Cleveland was a prominent figure in Buffalo and was elected mayor, but he served only one year of his term as he was elected governor of New York that same year. As governor, based on the urging of Frederick Law Olmsted, in early 1883 Cleveland signed the first act allowing the creation of a state park around

Niagara Falls. Although not officially created until 1885 by then-governor David Hill, Cleveland cleared the way for establishing the country's first state park.

While serving as governor in 1884, Cleveland successfully ran for president of the United States. Functioning first as the rare bachelor head of state, he married Buffalo's Francis Folsom in 1886, becoming the only President to be married in the White House. Several years his junior, Folsom was the daughter of Cleveland's former law partner and a family friend for many years.

The 1888 election was a controversial one, for in it, Cleveland won the popular vote, but failed to carry enough states to win the Electoral College, leaving Benjamin Harrison the winner. In 1892, however, Cleveland was elected again as President, earning the distinction of being the only President to be elected to discontinuous terms.

Although Grover Cleveland was remembered most for the trivial aspects of his terms in office, he was actually well respected by common citizens and disliked by big business and political rings. In one of his most controversial moves, he forced several railroad companies to return to the government 81 million acres of land in the West.

Unlike Fillmore, Cleveland did not return to Buffalo when he left office, choosing instead to move back to New Jersey. He never forgave the citizens of Buffalo for raising a scandal during his campaign, and although he did have some friends here, he refused to return. He died in Princeton in 1908.

Not an American President, but perhaps better known nationally than both Fillmore and Cleveland, Samuel Clemens (whose pen name was Mark Twain) spent several years in Buffalo during this time. Clemens moved to Buffalo in 1869 to become editor of one of the leading newspapers, the *Morning Express*. Although he and his family only lived in the splendid mansion at 472 Delaware avenue until moving again in 1871, Buffalo still identifies strongly with Clemens. The Buffalo and Erie County Public Library has an extensive Twain collection and a new Mark Twain Museum is slated to open in 2003.

Employing World-Class Design

Although only a few Buffalonians would go on to national and world fame, the influx of railroad money on top of the still strong canal shipping revenues allowed many in Buffalo to purchase world-class goods. It also motivated the city fathers to strive for the world-class amenities they could now afford. Among these were houses as palatial as those in New York City, paved streets in the major downtown areas, commercial buildings breaking the three-story barrier, and recreational areas for show and function.

In 1868, continuing the trend of bringing in noted architects and designers begun when St. Paul's hired Upjohn, the city fathers (including Pascal Pratt, Sherman Jewett, and William Dorsheimer) commissioned Frederick Law Olmsted and Calvert Vaux to design a comprehensive park system in Buffalo. This commission resulted in the first complete park and parkway system ever designed by the firm. Olmsted and Vaux were the first landscape architects in the country. In fact, they coined the term "landscape architect" to describe their work and "parkway" to describe their roadways.

Olmsted and Vaux's original park system was designed to connect three park areas to be used for various functions. Two small parks, Front and Parade, were designed to provide playgrounds, concert areas, and room for military exercises, while Delaware Park, more than 350 acres in size, was intended to be the ultimate quiet retreat from city life. Two of the parks employed water as part of their soothing nature. Front Park provided a spectacular view of the Niagara River, and in Delaware Park, Olmsted and Vaux created a lake. Building these parks and parkways would take the city eight years.

With the addition of a fountain and wading pool in 1896, the Parade was rechristened Humboldt Park. It was renamed again in 1978 to the current Martin Luther King Park. Most of Front Park was lost to the ramps and access areas of the Peace Bridge, opened in 1927.

In Olmsted and Vaux's original design, wide parkways connected these three parks to one another and to the downtown area. The placement of Delaware Park led to increased development of grand mansions along Delaware Avenue from downtown, as well as development on the adjoining streets, especially West Ferry, Richmond, Elmwood, and Linwood. As Charles West remembers the street in 1851, prior to the building of the park, Delaware had not been paved, nor did it have sidewalks other than "broken plank." It had none of the 2,100 gas lamps, just "a few miserable oil-lamp lights [that] served to make the darkness more hideous." It also had a soap factory, lumber yard, brick yard, and lead factory, and "scarcely a house of any pretension was to be found."

But after the park opened, the situation changed immensely. "Then, the Avenue led nowhere but to the swamps of Scajaquada Creek and the more desolate lands beyond, but now it leads to the beautiful city of the dead and to the lovely Park with its pathways, its serpentine walks, its romantic lake and miniature islands, and its expansive lawns dotted with umbrageous oaks of a century's growth." And once Delaware Avenue went somewhere, it became the most glamourous residential street in the city. "The wand of the fairy magician has wrought its wondrous transformation! Palatial residences, with their beautiful parterres of flowers and evergreens, have sprung up, the admiration of the stranger." This development continued along Delaware well into the twentieth century.

While monitoring the implementation of his park system plans, Olmsted was commissioned for two small jobs in the 1870s. In 1874, he designed the grounds in Niagara Square and, in 1876, the grounds of the new city and county hall. Olmsted also laid out a residential plan for the area east of Delaware Park, thought to be the first such plan in the country. A major development company purchased the land and created Olmsted's curvilinear streets, turning Parkside into the next "in" place for Buffalo's wealthy to reside.

Olmsted returned to Buffalo to design Cazenovia and South Parks in South Buffalo in 1887, and his firm designed Riverside Park in 1898. The complete plans for these parks were never fully realized and many of the most attractive features in each have been removed. Even so, Olmsted's influence on the city was great. The original three parks—Delaware, Humboldt, and Front with 365, 56, and 48 acres respectively—and the new parks—South, Cazenovia, and Riverside with 155, 106, and 22 acres—were major draws to their areas. After the creation of Riverside Park, minor areas, such as Niagara Square, combined with the major parks to bring the city's parkland total to 1,052 acres.

As an unknown admirer said of the Buffalo park system nearly a century ago, "In respect to the more quiet, tranquilizing and simply wholesome and refreshing forms of recreation—in beauty of water, meadow and woodland, which is the soul of a park—Buffalo has already more and is much faster gaining value than New York."

Just one year after Olmsted was first brought to Buffalo, in 1869, a young H.H. Richardson designed a house for New York State Lieutenant Governor William Dorsheimer. William was the son of Philip and continued his father's success in politics. The Dorsheimer House at 434–438 Delaware Avenue was so early in Richardson's career that it predates his use of Romanesque, an architectural style whose revival is so associated later with Richardson that to this day it is called "Richardsonian Romanesque." The Dorsheimer house is considered to be a French Neo-Grec design, and it is likely that Dorsheimer's pleasure in this building helped Richardson gain commissions for both the State Capitol in Albany and the Buffalo State Hospital (Buffalo State Psychiatric Center). Dorsheimer's former home is now a commercial property and is listed on the National Register of Historic Places.

The National Historic Landmark original Buffalo State Hospital building Richardson designed in 1871 is considered by some architectural historians to be the first Richardson building in the Romanesque style that would later bear his name. The hospital is a massive red Medina sandstone complex actually built in stages and was said to have kept Richardson's small office afloat during the 1873 depression. The first stage, the administration building and some patient facilities, was completed in 1880, while the full complex was not completed until 1895, nine years after Richardson's death. The dominant features of the administration building are its twin towers, more than eight stories high (185 feet) and visible for miles.

The grounds of the center were designed by Olmsted and Vaux, who continued to work frequently with Richardson after this first pairing. The grounds, originally encompassing more than 200 acres, were designed to be functional as well as beautiful. The park-like sections of the grounds included walking paths and gardens, while the land to the east running to the former Scajacuada Creek was farmland. The farm was used for growing produce for the patients, as well as for providing them with additional recreation.

Much later in his career, in 1886, Richardson returned to Buffalo to design a house for William H. Gratwick, a lumber and shipping baron. This house was also located on Delaware Avenue, Buffalo's prime residential street for much of the late nineteenth and twentieth centuries. The Gratwick House was at 776 Delaware Avenue on the corner of Summer and is said to have been Richardson's last commission before his untimely death in 1886. It was a Romanesque stone mansion, torn down in 1919 for the parking lot of the Red Cross.

Continuing in the quest for great designs, the city held a design competition when it decided to build a new public library building. The library had been operating as a private collection through the Young Men's Association since its founding in 1835. By 1886 the amassed collection was nearly 300,000 books in search of a larger storage facility. Although H.H. Richardson submitted plans to the competition, the commission went to Cyrus Eidlitz. Eidlitz was the son of Leopold Eidlitz, also a renowned architect who had worked with Richardson on the state capital. Romanesque in style and completed in 1887, the Buffalo Public Library building was Cyrus Eidlitz's first major commission. It launched his own successful career, leading to his most famous building, the New York Times Building in New York City. Eidlitz's library building dominated Lafayette Square until 1961 when it was torn down for the nondescript current library.

Buffalo as a Railroad Mecca

Although the railroads arrived in Buffalo in the 1830s, it was from 1850 through 1890 that these iron transportation giants turned Buffalo into a railroad mecca. Although most of these lines no longer exist, a brief look at their development shows how they helped spur Buffalo's growth.

In 1852, several railroads opened to Buffalo, with the most important perhaps the connection of the New York and Erie Railway from New York City. This line opened to Lake Erie in Dunkirk in 1851 and Buffalo was added to the line in two ways. The first was via the Buffalo and Attica Railroad, which had recently been extended to Hornellsville (Hornell). The second access point was through another line running from Buffalo directly to Corning known as the Buffalo, Corning and New York Railroad. According to the Galesburg Railroad Museum, "The earliest known use of a caboose as a word was in 1855, and it referred to the Conductor's car. This was on the Buffalo, Corning & New York Railroad, a predecessor of Erie-Lackawana and Conrail." The New York and Erie Railway later became the New York, Lake Erie, and Western Railroad.

Other roads finished in 1852 were the Buffalo and Rochester Railroad, the Buffalo and State Line Railroad along the south shore of Lake Erie and on to Chicago, and the Buffalo and Brantford. The Rochester to Batavia section of the Buffalo and Rochester line had already been operating for some time but the section west of Batavia was not done until 1852. This line became part of the New York Central in 1853. The Buffalo and State Line and other connecting lines switched to uniform rail gauges in 1854 and later became the Lake Shore and Michigan Southern Railroad. The name of the Buffalo and Brantford was changed to the Buffalo and Lake Huron in 1858.

In the 1860s much of the railroad news came in consolidations rather than in new lines. The most pertinent mergers both occurred in 1869. The New York Central Railroad merged with the Hudson River Railroad, calling the new line, not surprisingly, the New York Central and Hudson River Railroad Company. West of Buffalo, many lines along the south shore of Lake Erie and on toward Chicago united to form the Lake Shore and Michigan Southern Company. During this same year, the combined grain shipments on these two lines surpassed those shipped via the Erie Canal.

Building new lines started again in 1870. The small Buffalo Creek Railroad running from William Street to the south side of Buffalo Creek opened in 1870 and in 1889 became part of the Erie and the Lehigh Valley railroad companies. In 1873, a line opened from Buffalo to Amherstburg, Ontario, southwest of Windsor, and was known as the Canada Southern Railway. In 1878 it became known as the Michigan Central Railroad Company.

A major improvement in travel was the opening, also in 1873, of the Buffalo and Washington Railway, which ran from town south to Emporium, Pennsylvania. Connecting there to other southeasterly lines, it made travel to Philadelphia and on to Washington, D.C. both shorter and more convenient. For a short time, this line was renamed the Buffalo, New York and Philadelphia and then became part of the Pennsylvania Railroad.

In 1870, the Buffalo and Lake Huron line was leased to a Canadian line, the Grand Trunk Railway Company. In 1873–1874, this same group built the first bridge over the Niagara River, which still stands today about a mile north of the Peace Bridge.

The last new line opened in the 1870s was known as the Buffalo and Jamestown. First opened in 1875, then sold in 1877 and renamed the Buffalo and Southwestern Railroad, it connected Buffalo to Jamestown, New York. In 1881 it became part of the New York, Lake Erie and Western Railroad.

Additional rail connections in the 1880s included the New York, Chicago, and St. Louis through to Chicago in 1882; the New York, Lackawanna and Western connecting the Delaware, Lackawanna and Western to Buffalo from Binghamton, also in 1882; the Buffalo, Pittsburgh, and Western, running from Brocton to Buffalo to connect with the Oil City and Franklin in 1883; the Buffalo, Rochester, and Pittsburgh, connecting to the Rochester and Pittsburgh in 1883; the Lehigh Valley line, running on the Erie tracks, opened in 1884; and the West Shore Railroad in 1885. By 1887, 11 separate lines ran to Buffalo.

INVENTION AND INDUSTRY

Based primarily still upon the commerce generated by the Erie Canal, the growth of industry in Buffalo by 1860 was accelerating. By this time, it was already the second largest place of commerce in the state, with the full gamut of manufacturing, shipping, retail, and service-related businesses.

One of the most important to the city, especially in light of the numerous cholera outbreaks, was the public water system. As J.H. French describes it in his popular 1860 *New York State Gazetteer*:

> The main part of the city is supplied with wholesome water from Niagara
> River by the Buffalo Water Works Company. The reservoir, situated on

Niagara between Connecticut and Vermont Sts., is 88 ft. higher than the river, and has a capacity of 13,500,000 gallons. The water is elevated by two force pumps, each of a capacity of 235 gallons, and is distributed through 31 mi. of pipe.

By this time the harbor had also expanded to a 10-acre area including two basins, the Erie and the Ohio, and a main ship canal over a mile in length. With this additional capacity, local business ventures continued to evolve and companies relocated here throughout the decades from 1850 to 1890.

The number of grain elevators quickly increased from Dart's single elevator in 1842 to nearly 30 by 1864. The larger elevators could hold 600,000 bushels of grain for a total capacity of 6 million bushels in all the elevators. This increase in total capacity and the speed of the newer elevators allowed the Buffalo port to clear more grain in a day than it was able to do in the entire year in 1842. This not only exponentially increased the profits in Buffalo, but lowered the cost of grain shipping to less than one percent of previous costs. The ripple effect lowered the cost of grain-related products nationwide.

Shipping continued to be strong during this time, even though the war caused many of the southern Mississippi River ports to be closed to traffic. Despite this, dockworker and railroad worker strikes throughout the later 1800s often closed the port. One of the most violent occurred in the summer of 1863 when approximately 1,000 workers struck. The mostly Irish dockworkers were replaced by African Americans, and the dockworkers stormed the replacements' homes in retaliation, but were finally sent home by the militia. In 1877, similar violence broke out with railroad workers. Disgruntled laborers uncoupled train cars, put grease on the railroad tracks, and pulled out switches until volunteers and the militia arrived. Eight of the strikers were killed and an equal number of the militia were wounded in the confrontation.

Still, these occasional problems did not have much of an effect on the city's overall prosperity. What did affect it, though, in 1889, was the widening on the Sault Ste. Marie Canal. And this was in a positive way, for with a larger canal came larger ships that could bypass other Midwest ports. Doing so made shipping iron ore directly to Buffalo cheaper than shipping it to Pittsburgh. This set the stage for the tremendous growth of the steel industry in the twentieth century.

Another budding industry in Buffalo during this era was brewing. In 1859, one of Buffalo's largest and best known breweries, the John Schusler Brewing Company, was formed. The name was changed to the William Simon Brewery in 1899 when William

Simon, former brewmaster, bought out his partners, the surviving Schuslers. By 1872, Buffalo would be home to more than 35 breweries but only the Simon one would still be open 100 years later. It closed in 1973.

Theaters were also developing at a rapid pace, becoming not just recreation but thriving businesses. In 1842, there had been just one theater. That first theater had been opened in 1835 on Eagle Street and was appropriately named the Eagle Street Theater. Replete with painted Buffalo and a likeness of Red Jacket, the decor was said to have symbolized the rising of the city, which seems fitting for the first building in the city to be lighted with gas.

But while this first theater had been quaint, the newer theaters were impressive. This was certainly true of the Metropolitan Theatre/Academy of Music. Built in 1852, the Metropolitan Theatre was located on Main near Seneca. Built by Henry Meech, who also built an opera house in Rochester, its name was changed in 1868 (or 1870) when Meech's sons took over the business. In 1882, the building was extensively remodeled, with the entrance moved to Main Street, and the building raised to three stories on the Main Street side and four stories on the Washington Street side. The building was demolished *c.* 1955.

One of the most unique "theaters" during this time was the Cyclorama. This building, still located on Franklin Street, is a large "round" brick building built in 1888 to house a series of paintings showing a panoramic view of important historic events. Buildings like the Cyclorama were already popular in London and Paris when the builder of the Buffalo Cyclorama decided to bring this type of media display to the Queen City. The "round" building is actually a hexadecagon (16-sided), 130 feet in diameter and 92 feet high. To achieve the panoramic effect, paintings were hung in chronological order, which the patrons could view virtually simultaneously by standing around an elevated center column.

The original paintings displayed in the Buffalo Cyclorama were created by a French painter and depicted the city of Jerusalem during the crucifixion of Christ. These paintings hung for two years, drawing thousands of people to the Cyclorama. They were then replaced by a series of paintings depicting the Battle of Gettysburg. Unfortunately for the original owners of the Cyclorama, this type of art went out of vogue quickly, and after the Battle of Gettysburg show finished its own two year run, the building was closed.

The building's first true Renaissance started 40 years later, in 1937, courtesy of a Works Progress Administration (WPA) project to restore it as a library storage facility. The building had been assumed by the Grosvenor Library in 1913 and since then it had been used in a haphazard manner for storage. The WPA project cost less than $40,000 and transformed the Cyclorama into a beautiful building, so beautiful, in fact, that rather than use it for storage, the library decided to use it as a reading room. In this first adaptive use, the building got a new roof and a new floor. Windows were also added and the brick was repaired. It operated as a library reading room from 1942 until the library was closed in 1963. The main library building was razed, but the Cyclorama was saved. It went through hard times again for the next 20 years until it was converted in 1985–1989 to its current incarnation as an office building.

Just northeast of Olmsted's Delaware Park, a theater of a completely different type, the Buffalo Zoological Gardens, was opened in 1875. The elephant house was designed by local architects Augustus C. Esenwein and James A. Johnson, and in addition to the elephants, the zoo included bear, buffalo, seal, and other typical zoo animals. The zoo covers about 17 acres and has changed very little over the years.

Also geared toward arts entertainment, the Buffalo Fine Arts Academy was founded in 1862. After displaying its collection in a variety of places over the next 25 years, the collection was moved into the new Buffalo Public Library in 1887. In 1900, John Albright donated money toward a permanent home for the collection. On the southeast edge of Delaware Park, the white marble Albright Art Gallery opened in 1905. When noted art collector Seymour Knox died and left his collection to the academy, a new wing was added. Designed by Gordon Bunshaft of the New York City firm Skidmore, Owings and Merrill, the addition was opened in 1962. The gallery was then renamed the Albright-Knox Art Gallery.

To get to and from these venues, work, and school in these early years, citizens originally walked or rode in horse-drawn wagons. This started to change in the 1850s with the introduction of an "omnibus" line of horse-drawn streetcars. The original line ran up Main Street from the docks to what was known as the Cold Spring District, near Ferry. By 1863, there were approximately 60 cars operating on 11 miles of track. After 1875, special cars called "Main-Zoo-Cars" took visitors to the zoo. The cars continued to be horse-drawn, however, until 1882 when some were replaced by battery-driven engines. In 1889, five electric trolley cars started running to Delaware Park, and in 1896 the Buffalo system became the first totally electric system in the country.

Several businesses established during this time would become major players in Buffalo's and the nation's history. In 1852, Buffalo's William Fargo partnered with Henry Wells and founded what would later be known as Wells, Fargo & Co. Originally designed as a fast stage line from New York City to San Francisco, California, the company helped open up the West. Fargo was born in 1818 and had moved to

BUFFALO

Buffalo in 1843. He served as mayor of Buffalo from 1862 to 1865 and lived in a huge mansion on Fargo Avenue, named for him.

Two important banks were founded during this time. The first was the Erie County Savings Bank, incorporated in 1854 and run by William Bird until his death in 1878. The other, founded in 1856, was Manufacturers and Traders Trust, a commercial bank organized by Bronson Rumsey and Pascal Pratt to provide loans to the growing manufacturing businesses. Still one of the leading businesses in Buffalo today, more than 100 years after its initial founding, this bank's corporate headquarters, designed by Minoru Yamasaki, is of national importance.

One of the most unique businesses of this time was the medical-related business of Dr. Ray Vaughn Pierce. Pierce ran the Invalid Hotel and Surgical Institute out of a grand brick building at 663 Main Street. Many famous people came to recuperate at Pierce's hotel during its heyday, including, supposedly, the Sundance Kid. Pierce also ran the World's Dispensary, a six-story manufacturing facility on Washington. Pierce's medicines were notorious elixirs, many containing opium until the mid-1890s. Pierce promoted his concoctions through his book, *The People's Common Sense Medical Adviser*. A quasi-predecessor to the *Physicians' Desk Reference*, Pierce's book was in its 11th edition and had sold more than 2 million copies by 1907.

Other important businesses in this era were the lumber businesses of William Gratwick and the Goodyear brothers, Charles and Frank, the stove business of Sherman Jewett, the wallpaper business of George Birge, the tanning businesses of brothers Dexter and Bronson Rumsey and Jacob Schoellkopf, the forge run by William and Henry Wendt, the breweries of Gerhard Lang and Magnus Beck, the bicycle and later auto business of George Pierce, the soap businesses of John D. Larkin and the Lautz Brothers, the banks of John Albright and Pascal Pratt, the retail stores of William Hengerer, Robert Adam, John Adam, Edward Kleinhans, and Seymour Knox, the flour mills of George Urban, the race track/driving park of Chauncey Hamlin, and the newspaper run by Edward Butler.

Charles Waterhouse Goodyear was the first of the Goodyear brothers to arrive in Buffalo. Born in 1846, he moved to Buffalo in 1868, working first in various law firms until he passed the bar in 1871. He practiced primarily in his own firm for more than 15 years, and also intermittently with a partner and in larger firms. In the late 1870s, he served several years as assistant district attorney, then district attorney, but by the end of the following decade, he had given up his legal career to become one of Buffalo's leading lumber barons.

Frank Henry Goodyear was three years younger than Charles and moved to Buffalo in 1872. In 1887, the brothers formed a lumber company called F.H. and

C.W. Goodyear. The company logged trees on several parcels in Pennsylvania and helped develop a railroad to ship the lumber. Their railroad, known as the Buffalo and Susquehanna Railroad, would grow to ship more than 400 million feet of lumber per year.

Both Goodyears were active in the community and, with John Albright, would later help bring the steel industry to Buffalo. They would each build beautiful mansions on Delaware Avenue, and Charles's mansion at 888 still stands. Frank died in 1907, while Charles lived until 1911.

George Birge was a native Buffalonian, born in 1849 to Martin Birge, owner and founder in 1834 of the M.H. Birge wallpaper company. Birge attended Cornell University and then returned to help run the family business. When his brother also joined the firm, the company name was changed to M.H. Birge and Sons. In 1890 the brothers sold the business, but bought it back again in 1900. Birge was a strong proponent of holding the Pan-American Exposition in Buffalo and, from 1908 to 1916, president of Pierce-Arrow. His mansion is extant at Symphony Circle.

William and Henry Wendt ran a forge company named Buffalo Forge. Opened by William in 1878 to make hand forges for blacksmiths, by the 1890s, the company had broadened the product line to include other metal-related components such as punches, shears, and rollers.

When George Urban opened his flour business in 1846, it was originally a traditional mill. By the late 1880s, the Urban Roller Mill on Ellicott and Oak Streets was a full-functioning roller mill, the first to use that technology in the city. Urban's sons George Jr. and William took over the company in 1885 and helped keep the mill one of the most popular with residential and commercial flour users. Their brands were known as "Pearl," "Bakers," and "Urban's Best."

Bronson Cage and Dexter Phelps Rumsey, sons of Aaron Rumsey, moved to Buffalo with their father and family in the early 1830s. Aaron opened a tannery and as the city grew, so did the business. Both brothers joined the firm and helped turn it into one of the largest tanning companies in the country. They later sold their business to United States Leather for purportedly $20 million, and each turned those millions to other investments, primarily railroads, real estate, and banks. Throughout the late 1800s, the brothers were clearly the leading businessmen in Buffalo, owning at one time more than half of the property in the city.

Together with the civic and other business leaders, these men helped shape the future of Buffalo, moving it firmly toward the twentieth century. While all this progress was generally good for the city, there were several associated disasters, too, most of which took the form of fires in hotels and other public places. Having been dealt such a severe blow by the burning of the village in 1813, firefighting measures were instituted early in the city's history. Soon after the rebuilding, citizens were supposed to keep leather buckets in their homes to make it easier to form bucket brigades as necessary. In 1817, the process was formalized into a volunteer fire company, still using just the leather buckets but in a more orderly manner.

The first traditional fire company, complete with fire engine, arrived in 1824. It was called Cataract Engine No. 1, and was followed seven years later by the first hook and ladder company, appropriately called Pioneer. In 1837, the first alarm bell was installed in the Terrace Market. The companies continued to grow throughout the mid-1800s and by 1859 included a brand new steam pumper, in addition to the 11 hand engines, 2 hook and ladders, and 12 hose companies.

In 1880, the fire department switched from volunteer to paid professional firefighters. The city had tried unsuccessfully to do this in both 1862 and 1872, but was able to do so this time largely due to the increased threat of fires in the grain elevators proliferating along the water front. This also necessitated a way to reach the more remote elevators, so in 1887, the fire department bought its first fireboat. By 1900, there were three such fireboats in service.

Unfortunately, none of this stopped the devastating fires. One of the worst fires was the Clarendon Hotel fire in November 1860. This hotel had been located on the corner of Main and South Division Streets. Five years later, three men were killed in the American Hotel fire in 1865. This building had been on Main just north of Eagle.

The next major fire was not a hotel but a factory. In December 1880, the M.H. Birge & Sons factory burned to the ground. Located on Perry Street, the company had been a wallpaper manufacturer. As it went, it took the Queen City Malt House with it. Ten people died.

In March of 1885, the new Music Hall on Main Street burned down due to an ignited gas leak. Because the water mains had frozen, the fire department could not contain the flames. They spread to the St. Louis Church next door, burning it to the ground, too. Two men died in this fire, but miraculously, none of the attendees at the show in progress in the Music Hall nor those in the service at St. Louis were injured. In fact, the St. Louis parishioners had time to remove many of the furnishings from the building before it was consumed.

Continued on page 97

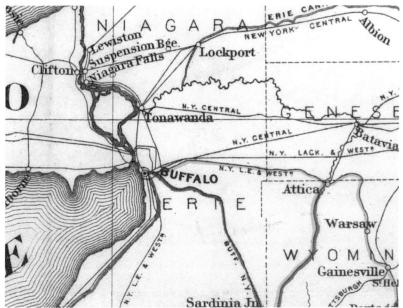

MAP OF WESTERN NEW YORK. *This excerpt of a map of the Pittsburgh Railroad system shows Buffalo's relation to Lake Erie, Lake Ontario, and the rest of Western New York.*

OLD COURT HOUSE. *While the original courthouse was burned during the war, this one stood on Lafayette Square for 60 years.*

ERIE CANAL. *Mules tow a barge along the Erie Canal in Buffalo, probably dating to the late 1800s.*

1838 SCHOOL. In 1912, this school was the oldest school building in the city. It is now demolished.

*1833 L*IGHTHOUSE. *A closeup of the 1833 lighthouse dates from the early 1900s.*

AMERICAN BLOCK FIRE. *This photo shows the damage to the American Hotel and surrounding buildings caused by the 1865 fire.*

BLIZZARD OF *1888. The Blizzard of 1977 and the back-to-back storms of 2001 were not the only large snowfalls in the city's history.*

ELMWOOD MUSIC HALL. *Originally the 74th Regiment Armory, this building was designed by Buffalo's Louise Bethune. It stood on the corner of Elmwood and Virginia, next to the relocated Coit House, and functioned as the city's prime music hall until Kleinhans opened in 1940.*

FIRST PRESBYTERIAN CHURCH. *Founded in 1812, the congregation of the First Presbyterian Church is the oldest in the city. This wonderful drawing commemorating the church's official incorporation in 1827 shows the three buildings occupied by the church prior to its move to Symphony Circle in 1891.*

HUMBOLDT PARK. *This view of a garden in Humboldt Park, originally named "The Parade" by Olmsted, shows what is today known as Martin Luther King, Jr. Park.*

JACK BROWN'S BUFFET. Located at 15 Oak Street, this tavern was one of the many in Buffalo in the mid- to late 1800s.

IROQUOIS HOTEL. One of the largest hotels in the city when it opened in 1889, it proclaimed itself "fireproof," no doubt since it occupied the previous site of the YMA/Richmond Hotel, which burned in 1887. Note the top floors, added to the new Richmond for the Pan-American Exposition in 1901.

MASONIC TEMPLE. *The Buffalo Masons were one of the largest fraternal organizations in the city with more than 4,000 members. This was their new headquarters.*

OLD TEMPLE BETH ZION. *This temple was opened on Delaware Avenue in 1889. It was used until a devastating fire in the 1960s.*

OLD MUSIC
HALL. *This
music hall burned
in 1885, taking
St. Louis Church
with it.*

ORIGINAL M&T BANK.
*This modest building housed the
Manufacturers and Traders Bank for
much of the mid-1800s.*

BUFFALO PUBLIC LIBRARY. *Cyrus Eidlitz's masterpiece, demolished in 1961 to build the current nondescript library building.*

SHELTON SQUARE IN THE 1880S. *Note the middle church, which is St. Joseph's Church. Both St. Paul's and St. Joseph's still stand, but the Prudential and other later buildings now rise between them. This reproduction is from* The Picture Book of Earlier Buffalo, *published by the Buffalo Historical Society.*

NEW YORK STATE HOSPITAL. *H.H. Richardson's massive hospital is now a National Historic Landmark.*

ST. LOUIS CHURCH. *The oldest Catholic church in Buffalo, this shows the building rebuilt after the 1885 fire.*

ST. LOUIS INTERIOR. *The interior of St. Louis is shown as rebuilt after the 1885 fire.*

BUFFALO IN 1896. *This map shows the city as it was in 1896. Note the open parklands in Delaware Pak and around the state hospital near the top center of the map.*

BROADWAY MARKET. *Here as it looked in the early twentieth century, the Broadway Market is the only surviving market in Buffalo today. This building was replaced in the 1950s with the current building.*

DELAWARE AVENUE BAPTIST CHURCH. *This Richardsonian-Romanesque church was built in 1894 and is the major remaining work of Buffalo architect John Hopper Coxhead. Many of Buffalo's wealthiest citizens were members of this church, including Seymour Knox and Eric Hedstrom.*

BUFFALO HARBOR. *The harbor trade is what built the city in the 1800s, and the harbor continued to be an important part of commerce in the early 1900s. This view shows several of the grain elevators and boats docked at them.*

DELAWARE PARK BAND STAND. *Delaware Park was famous for its concerts, and this scene shows the crowds around the band stand.*

DELAWARE AVENUE. *Buffalo's premier residential street, this view shows what appears to be people on Sunday buggy rides and strolls under the canopy of shade trees.*

DR. PIERCE'S HOSPITAL. One of Buffalo's more notorious characters, Dr. Pierce sold elixirs laced with opium and ran this recovery hospital/hotel.

ELLICOTT SQUARE ATRIUM. This is an old view of the beautiful atrium over the main concourse in the Ellicott Square building.

ELLICOTT SQUARE. *When it opened in 1896, the Ellicott Square building was the largest office building in the world. Designed primarily by Charles Atwood with Daniel Burnham, the building was renovated in the 1980s.*

EXCHANGE STREET STATION. *New York Central's station on Exchange Street is pictured here as it appeared in the early 1900s.*

FIRST PRESBYTERIAN CHURCH. *The congregation of the First Presbyterian Church moved from its Shelton Square church into this new church at Symphony Circle in 1891. The church was designed by Green and Wicks and still dominates the circle. This is a current view, taken by the author.*

FIDELITY TRUST. *Fidelity Trust was one of the largest banks in Buffalo in the early 1900s.*

JOHNSON PARK. *The prime residential area in the mid- to late 1800s, it was replaced by Delaware Avenue when Elmwood Avenue was extended through the park. It still has one of the most eclectic collections of homes in the city.*

LAFAYETTE SQUARE. *One of the city's most prominent "squares," this view from the early 1900s shows, from left to right, the public library, Lafayette Hotel, and Brisbane Building, with the Soldiers and Sailors Monument in the center.*

FRONT PARK. One of Olmsted and Vaux's original three parks in the city, Front Park was still a popular resting place into the early 1900s.

LIVESTOCK EXCHANGE. Designed in 1892 by Louise Bethune, this building was the center of Buffalo's livestock business well into the 1900s.

NIAGARA AND FRANKLIN. *These are the buildings at the intersection of Niagara Street and Franklin Street in the early 1900s. On the far right is City and County Hall, and in the distant center, St. Joseph's Church.*

Strength, Speed, Simplicity, Symmetry

are distinctive properties of Pierce Motorcycles.

The life of a motorcycle is in its frame and engine.

THE Pierce Frame is constructed of steel tubing 3¼" in diameter. It will not break or buckle and is built to stand all kinds of rough roads and hard use. Broken frames, the cause of frequent complaint in other motorcycles, are unknown in the Pierce.

¶ The Pierce Single has a 5 H. P. four cycle engine, fitted with roller bearings, mechanical valves, magneto ignition and free engine clutch. *This is also made to last*, not being of the excessively high speed type. Although not intended for racing, it has a speed of 55 miles an hour and power to climb hills that other singles cannot. The Pierce Single is a motorcycle with the power and road strength of a twin cylinder and the serviceability and simplicity of a single. A maximum of efficiency and a minimum of trouble and expense for repairs.

¶ This company also manufactures the famous Pierce Four Cylinder, the most complete motorcycle made. Also Pierce Bicycles famous for over twenty years, and ridden by all the well-known racing men.

Motorcycle catalogue "LF" on application.

The Pierce Cycle Company :: :: Buffalo, N. Y.

PIERCE MOTORCYCLE. *This advertisement is for one of the motorcycles produced by the Pierce Cycle Company, predecessor to the Pierce-Arrow car company.*

New Post Office. Just east of Ellicott Square, the new post office also had an atrium area. This building is now used as Erie Community College's main city campus building.

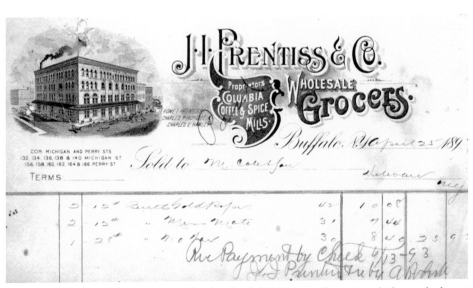

PRENTISS COMPANY. *This 1893 billhead is for the J.I. Prentiss Company, which was the largest wholesale grocery company in Buffalo at that time. The building burned in 1922 and the site is now a parking lot for the HSBC Arena.*

SHELTON SQUARE. *This is perhaps the most recognizable view of Buffalo all throughout the late 1890s and into the 1960s. From left to right, St. Paul's Church, the Prudential Building, and George Post's 1890 Erie County Savings Bank.*

WATER SPORTS. *Recreational boating was very popular in Buffalo during this era. This shows the crowds on the docks at a boating event.*

ELECTRIC TOWER AT NIGHT. *The most spectacular part of the Pan-American Exposition was the lighting in the evenings. This is how the Electric Tower and surrounding buildings looked at night.*

HISTORICAL SOCIETY BUILDING. *The New York State Building at the Pan-American was the only building designed to be a permanent Buffalo building after the fair. This building still houses the Buffalo and Erie County Historical Society.*

MILBURN HOUSE. *This was John Milburn's house, where McKinley was taken to recuperate after being shot. Unfortunately, he also died here.*

WILCOX HOUSE. *Owned by Ansley Wilcox, this is the home in which Teddy Roosevelt took the oath of office for President after McKinley died. It is now a National Historic Site.*

PAN-AMERICAN TRIUMPHAL BRIDGE. *This bridge went over Mirror Lake, connecting the south portion of the grounds to the north portion.*

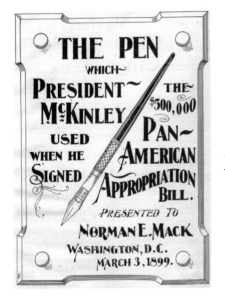

PAN-AMERICAN PEN. *This advertisement for the Pan-American proudly displays a drawing of the pen McKinley used to sign the federal appropriation for the fair. The pen was later presented to a contest winner.*

PAN-AMERICAN ELEPHANT. *This humorous picture shows an attendee to the fair giving a glass of beer to an elephant while the trainer watches.*

COURT STREET. *A c.1920s view down Court Street shows the old Shea's Theater with the McKinley Monument in the distance.*

EARLY SNOWMOBILE. *This intriguing view is of some men in front of a truck rigged with treads and skis to "snowmobile" on the lake.*

THOMAS CAR ADVERTISEMENT. One of Buffalo's most famous car companies, the Thomas Motor Car Company was founded in 1902. This advertisement is from 1911, shortly before the plant closed.

CITY HALL. *Designed by local architects Dietel and Wade, the present City Hall is an imposing art deco building dominating Niagara Square. It was started in 1929 and opened in 1931. In the foreground is the McKinley Monument, built in 1907. Current photograph by the author.*

Continued from page 64

More terrible than this conflagration, though, was the Richmond Hotel fire in March 1887. Located at the corner of Main south of Eagle, this fire killed 15 and injured more than 30. The telephone and telegraph wires strung on poles along the street were blamed for the firemen's inability to reach the higher floors. This prompted the city to make the communications companies move all the wiring underground. The side benefit to this was the greatly enhanced beauty of the streets. The new Richmond Hotel was designed by Cyrus Eidlitz, who also designed the first Buffalo Public Library.

To provide the growing city with produce and other goods, four large markets were built in Buffalo in the mid-nineteenth century. These markets were bustling centers for retail activities in the various sections of the city well into the 1900s. Built in 1845, the Elk Street Market was located in the southeastern part of the city, running along Elk Street. It was 30 feet wide and 375 feet long, with verandas 24 feet wide extending the full length of both sides. The Clinton Street Market was located on Clinton Street and was similar to the Elk Street Market, with a 36 foot wide by 395 foot long main building, also sporting 24 foot wide verandas on each side. In the northeast section of downtown, the Washington Street Market was an exact copy of the Clinton Street Market, running along Washington Street from Chippewa halfway to Tupper to where St. Michael's is still today. The most unique market in town was the Court Street Market. The main building was 51 feet square, with 36 foot wide wings extending north, south, east, and west. The north and south wings were 91 feet long and the east and west wings were 61 feet long.

In 1888, a fifth market was born. Located at 999 Broadway, this is the only market still in operation in Buffalo. Although on its third building dating to the 1950s, this market is still a popular place, especially during the Easter and Christmas seasons.

ENHANCING THE COMMUNITY

The community services needed by the expanding population continued to increase. From the one post office established in 1804 sprang five by 1860. One was in the downtown area, and the other four were in the outlying areas known then as Buffalo Plains, North Buffalo, Red Jacket, and the former village of Black Rock.

As the population grew and businesses expanded, it became clear that the city also needed to provide a variety of educational opportunities to the residents. Partially endowed through a $10,000 donation from Jabez Goodell, the Buffalo Female Academy on Delaware was established in 1851. As French described in 1866, "The academy occupies one of the most eligible and beautiful sites in the city." The school changed its name to The Buffalo Seminary in 1889 and in 1908 moved to its current location at Bidwell Parkway and Potomac Avenue.

Two business colleges, the Buffalo Mercantile College and the Buffalo Commercial College, were created to help teach business and entrepreneurship to new and existing residents. The former was created in 1854.

The public schools were growing, too. When the city was incorporated in 1832, six part-time fee-based schools existed. In 1837, a Board of Education and city school superintendent position were created. This was purportedly the first full-time city school superintendent job in the country. The schools also became free, although this continued to be an issue for many years.

By 1857, the number of schools had increased more than five-fold to 32, serving approximately 16,000 students with 189 teachers. In addition to the elementary schools, the first dedicated high school was formed in 1852. Named Central High School, this school operated out of a converted mansion at Franklin and Court. An addition in 1869 and another in 1889 expanded the original mansion considerably, allowing this single facility to function as the only city high school until 1897.

Public service organizations were also important to the city during these years. One of the most important was the Young Men's Christian Union, formed in Buffalo in 1852. Part of the international group started in London in 1844, the Buffalo chapter was the third in North America, following the Montreal and Boston chapters. In 1868, the organization's name changed to the Young Men's Christian Association (YMCA). In 1887, it sold its building, which was remodeled into the Richmond Hotel. Unfortunately, this hotel would burn just months later.

As noted in the previous chapter, Roman Catholic Bishop John Timon was active in bringing several groups to Buffalo to establish religious organizations for the many Catholic immigrants. One of the first was St. Mary's School for the Deaf, organized in 1853. A school on Edward Street was built in 1862 and enlarged five times by 1880. By 1873, the school would provide free education to the deaf via state and county programs. The property on Main and Dewey was purchased in 1883 and a frame building completed. In 1898, the current building was finished and there were more than 150 students in the program.

In 1870, several German Jesuits arrived and founded Canisius College on Ellicott Street. Founded in 1540 by Spain's Saint Ignatius Loyola, the Jesuits are a Roman Catholic order formally known as The Society of Jesus. Named after St. Peter

Canisius, who was a Dutch Jesuit from the 1500s, Canisius was the first Catholic college in the city. It relocated to a new building at the corner of Washington and Tupper in 1872. Canisius High School was founded at the same time. Both the school and college operated out of the Washington Street building until 1912, when the college moved into Old Main at its present location on Main Street. In 1944, work was started on the present Canisius High School on Delaware. While some students attended school at that location the following year, the full student body did not relocate there until 1948.

But Bishop Timon wasn't the only person concerned with the wellness aspects of life in Buffalo. Another strong proponent of social welfare during this era was Maria Love. A wealthy Buffalo native born in 1840, Love was deeply concerned with the effects of poverty and the urban environment on people. In 1879, Benjamin Fitch donated his property at 159 Swan Street for Love to provide community services. In 1880, she opened the doors of the Fitch Creche, said to be the first daycare center in the country. At the center, widows and other women forced to work to make ends meet were allowed to leave their children while at work. This saved many families from a life in "the poorhouse," or worse, children being taken from their mothers and placed in an orphanage.

Love's Fitch Creche became a model implemented in several other cities around the world. She continued to operate the center until her death in 1931. The building then functioned as a rooming house and was vacant for many years before being demolished in 1998.

Other public service institutions included two new hospitals. A small maternity hospital, the Lying-In Hospital, was opened by the Sisters of Charity on Edward Street. The larger hospital was the Buffalo General Hospital. Founded in 1855 with a $10,000 state grant and $20,000 in individual donations, this hospital opened in 1858. It was a two-story brick building, 75 feet wide and 160 feet long with two wings, each with four wards that held about 400 patients.

Buffalo's churches continued to evolve from 1850 through 1890. Many of the churches established from 1825 to 1850 expanded and built new brick or stone edifices. Many more new churches were created as the ethnic and religious mix of older neighborhoods changed and as new neighborhoods were created. By 1860, Buffalo had a population of 81,129, and French's *Gazetteer of New York* was boasting of the 57 churches in Buffalo that "most of the church edifices are large and commodious; and many of them are of a high order of architectural beauty."

The denomination with the most churches (14) was Roman Catholicism. These included St. Joseph's Cathedral, St. Louis, and St. Patrick's, as well as St. Ann's and

St. Michael's noted earlier. According to French, St. Joseph's was the biggest and most expensive church in the city in the 1860s. Opened in 1851, the large stone building included an altar window designed and built in Munich for $5,000. Located on Franklin and Swan Streets, the church was 236 feet long with a ceiling 75 feet high. The main portion of the church was 86 feet wide and 120 feet at the transept. The spire was 220 feet tall and was to hold the third largest carillon in the world. This church was replaced with the New St. Joseph's Cathedral on Delaware Avenue, but the old church was not torn down. This turned out to be a good thing, as the new church is now demolished and the old church has recently gone through a major restoration.

In the years before 1850 there was growing disharmony among the parishioners who had remained in the St. Louis Church, their pastor, trustees, and the new Bishop Timon. Apparently, the bishop wanted the church and land ceded to the diocese, and the church trustees refused. Things got so out of hand that, as one author states, "[it] raised such a commotion that the church administrative council was banned in 1851 and an interdiction was placed against the church." Four years later, though, a Father F. Wenninger was able to smooth things over, a new pastor, Father Deiters, was appointed, and church life ran relatively well until the 1835 brick building burned down on March 25, 1885. The congregation managed to stay together, however, and built the impressive stone structure still on Main and Edward today. This new church was dedicated in 1889 and is said to have the only remaining open stonework spire in the country.

Another large ethnic Catholic church built in 1882 was St. Stanislaus Church at 123 Townsend Street. Founded by Jan Pitass, who was also its pastor for 39 years, this church helped coalesce the newly arriving Polish immigrants. At its peak, it had one of the largest congregations in the country with 20,000 members. In addition to the church, Pitass set up a parish school that same year and opened a Polish cemetery in 1889. The towers of the church, completed in 1908, are still visible from virtually everywhere in the old Polish east side.

The Jesuits under Bishop Timon's direction also founded a church on Emslie at Broadway in 1848 known as St. Ann's and St. Michael's in 1851. The original St. Ann's was built in 1858. In 1878, construction started on a new building, which was opened in 1886. St. Michael's moved to its Washington Street location in 1864 and the present building was completed in 1870.

The second largest denomination by the 1860s was Presbyterianism with eight churches. Among the finest were the First Presbyterian on Shelton Square, North Presbyterian located on the southwest corner of Chippewa and Main, and Central

Presbyterian. In 1889, construction began on the present First Presbyterian Church on Symphony Circle. It was opened in 1891 and still is a dominant force in the neighborhood.

Tied for third with seven churches each were Protestant Episcopal and Methodist Episcopal. Six Baptist churches had been formed by 1860 and the remaining fifteen were a mix of denominations with four German Evangelical, three Lutheran, two Dutch Reformed, and one each of Unitarian, Universalist, French Protestant, Associated Presbyterian, Mission, and Bethel.

While many of these parishioners struggled to support themselves, they nonetheless found ways to contribute to their churches. This dedication to their churches and their new city would continue well into the twentieth century.

Chapter Six

GLORY DAYS

By 1890, Buffalo had grown to a population of more than 250,000. Manufacturing and supporting service businesses were booming, all prompting a corresponding rise both in the need for new commercial and residential buildings and the money with which to pay for them. In fact, many of the city's most prominent buildings hail from this era, as you will see from the explosive growth from the last decade of the nineteenth century through 1905.

CONTINUED GROWTH AND PROSPERITY

From the minimum required 10,000 people to become a city in 1832, the next 60 years saw Buffalo's population grow 25-fold to 255,664 in 1890. By 1895, Buffalo had 27 railroads with a combined total of 450 miles of track within the 42 square miles of the city. Improvements underway in 1895 created another 200 miles of railroad within the next few years.

The canal, lake, and railroad traffic combined to make Buffalo the sixth largest commercial city in the world in 1895, in terms of tonnage entered and cleared, and the third largest in the United States behind only New York City and Chicago. The city was the world's largest port in flour, wheat, and coal shipments and second only to Chicago in lumber. Considering that the weather allowed the port to remain open only an average of 246 days per year, this is truly remarkable.

And as the port prospered, the city grew. Both the increasing population and booming commerce had significant impact on the development of the city government as well as its schools and churches. The city's political subdivisions were increased from 5 to 13 wards in 1852 and in 1892 they were increased again to 25 wards. Other changes in the 1892 charter included lengthening the mayoral term to three years and creating nine council member at-large positions.

During this era Buffalo was not only a melting pot of religions, but also of ethnic groups and races. By far the largest immigrant group in Buffalo in the 1890s was still the Germans with 52,000 people, roughly 20 percent of the total population. The Irish were also still second, with 12,000, but gaining quickly was the third largest group, the Polish, with nearly 9,000. Much smaller, but still distinct, ethnic populations included the Italians with 2,500, Jewish with 1,500, and African Americans with 1,000.

Institutions and organizations continued to expand into the twentieth century. There were social clubs such as the Buffalo Club and the Phoenix Club (Jewish), charity groups such as the Buffalo Children's Aid Society and the Fitch Creche, and sports clubs such as the Buffalo Yacht Club. One of the most popular organizations was the Freemasons. In 1896, the Buffalo Freemasons had eleven lodges and four royal arch chapters with a total of more that 4,500 members, including several prominent business and political leaders.

Despite the nationwide depression of 1893, Buffalo prospered. During this unprecedented era of growth, the city's prominent citizens continued to look outside Buffalo for architects for their major projects. In fact, several of the nation's most celebrated architects designed buildings in Buffalo during this period. Daniel Burnham (with Charles Atwood as principal designer), Louis Sullivan, Frank Lloyd Wright, McKim, Mead & White, George Post, and Carrere & Hastings all designed Buffalo structures between 1890 and 1905.

Two major building commissions went to these out-of-towners in 1894. The first was the Ellicott Square Building, which went to Chicago-based Daniel Burnham & Company. Burnham had just gained national fame for his participation in the highly successful Chicago World's Fair, and the Ellicott Square Building helped build the career of his designer, Charles Atwood. Made with a terra cotta exterior, this ten story, 447,000 square foot building covers an entire city block in the prime central city area. In fact, it sits on the Main Street property Joseph Ellicott had purchased and saved for his unbuilt mansion.

When it opened in 1895, Ellicott Square was the largest office building in the world, containing 40 stores, 16 banking offices, and 600 other offices. Although now painted and missing its wonderful cornice, the Ellicott Square Building is extant. One of the most striking features remains the glass atrium above the beautiful mosaic main concourse floor.

Also in 1894, Chicago's Louis Sullivan was commissioned by Buffalonian Hascal L. Taylor to design an office building. Unfortunately Taylor died later that year, but the Guaranty Construction Company of Chicago took over the project and opened its new Guaranty Building in 1896. Around 1898, the Prudential Insurance Company refinanced the building and the name was changed to the Prudential Building, causing the continuing confusion over the building's name.

Sullivan's approach to the Guaranty/Prudential building varied greatly from Burnham and Atwood's Ellicott Square design. Situated on a much narrower lot,

Sullivan chose to make his building more vertical, with 13 stories. The Guaranty Building is generally acknowledged by Sullivan historians to be his finest work. It is also considered one of the first of the modern skyscrapers. The intricate elevator cages and internal support columns are among its most striking features. Some of the delicate ornamentation in the external terra cotta was designed by George Grant Elmslie, who, like Atwood, went on to have his own successful architectural career.

The Larkin Soap Company in the southeast area of Buffalo was, during this time, one of the largest mail order companies in the world. Founded by John D. Larkin in 1875, the company was one of the first direct-mail companies in the world. Originally selling products through the traditional retail outlets, in 1885 Larkin, a graduate of Buffalo's own Bryant and Stratton Business College, decided to cut out the middle man and sell directly to consumers. The company's trademark slogan was "Factory-to-Family," and to encourage customers to buy products in volume, Larkin created a bonus program that provided fairly expensive, high-quality furniture and other products as purchase incentives.

By the early 1900s, the Larkin Soap Company became the largest mail order company in the world and Larkin was ready to move all the company's administrative activities to a separate corporate building. In 1902, Darwin Martin, the company's chief financial officer, hired the little-known Chicago architect Frank Lloyd Wright, who had designed Martin's brother's Chicago home. The Larkin Administration Building was Wright's first commercial building and its boxy exterior, large open interior spaces, and specially-designed office furniture introduced a new style to office buildings. It contrasted with both the Ellicott Square and the Guaranty buildings. Its seven stories were constructed of reinforced concrete slabs, 10 inches thick, 17 feet wide, and 34 feet long placed on 24-inch steel girders.

The building cost $4 million to build. Unfortunately, the Larkin Company went bankrupt during the Depression and the city eventually acquired the property. The administration building was sold for $5,000 in 1949 and it was demolished in 1950 for a truck terminal that was never built.

Wright returned to Buffalo to design six more buildings between 1903 and 1929. The most famous of these is his Prairie Style house on Jewett Parkway near Delaware Park, which he designed for Larkin's Darwin Martin. To the Wright afficionados, the Martin house is the third most popular of all Wright's homes, especially noted for the "Tree of Life" pattern of the art glass used in the home. Banking on this pilgrimage appeal, the home is currently undergoing a $23 million restoration.

BUFFALO

All six of Wright's Buffalo residential designs were for executives in the Larkin company or relatives of Martin's. These include Martin's city residence, noted above, as well as Martin's summer house, known as Graycliff, in Derby, New York, south of Buffalo. The other four are the Barton House and Gardener's Cottage, actually part of the Martin estate complex, the Heath House, and the Davidson House.

But Chicago architects weren't the only ones being brought to Buffalo to create magnificent structures. In 1890, New York's George Post won the competition to design the Erie County Savings Bank. Opened in 1893, this massive Romanesque building shared the area known as Shelton Square with St. Paul's Church and the Guaranty Building. It was built of sandstone and was eight stories tall. Pre-dating both Ellicott Square and the Guaranty Building, it was one of the last and largest solid masonry buildings constructed in the city. It was demolished in 1967.

New York City architects McKim, Mead and White designed four mansions and a power plant in Buffalo. The Metcalfe Mansion, a large shingle style building once located at 125 North Street, near Delaware Avenue, was actually designed in 1882. In 1894, the firm returned to design the Root House at 650 Delaware Avenue and again in 1895 to design homes for Charles and George Williams at 672 and 690 Delaware Avenue. These Georgian Revival houses were in sharp contrast to the Victorian and Romanesque buildings on the street.

Combined with the Olmsted parks and Richardson buildings from the 1870s, the work of these out of town architects gave Buffalo an architectural heritage virtually unrivaled. Although the Post building is gone, the Richardson, Wright, and Sullivan buildings remain. Only three other cities in the United States (New York, Chicago, and St. Louis) had, and still have, an Olmsted park and buildings by Richardson, Sullivan, and Wright. And none of these three cities has more than one Richardson building or Buffalo's extensive park system. By bringing these important architects to town, Buffalo's major citizens succeeded in showing the rest of the country that the city was world-class.

By the 1890s, Buffalo also had its share of prominent local architects and firms, the most dominant of which was the firm of Green and Wicks. Edward Brodhead Green and his partner William S. Wicks moved to Buffalo from Auburn, New York in 1881. Green was a graduate of the Cornell School of Architecture and is still known today for his buildings on the campus of his alma mater. While Green & Wicks designed buildings outside the immediate Buffalo area, they are best known for their local buildings, including the Dun Building (1894–1895), the Buffalo

Savings Bank (1900–1901), and the Albright Art Gallery, opened in 1905. Green continued to practice in Buffalo in a variety of firms until 1950, when he died at the age of 94.

Another dominant force in Buffalo architecture during this era was the firm of Esenwein and Johnson. The firm is best known locally for its General Electric Building (1912) now known as the Niagara Mohawk Building. This white terra cotta building was supposedly inspired by the Electric Tower at the Pan-American Exposition. Esenwein and Johnson were nationally known hotel architects, designing the first Statler Hotel in Buffalo as well as large hotels in Boston and Cleveland. The most renowned building in their portfolio, however, was the Temple of Music at the Pan-American Exposition, in which President McKinley was assassinated.

Not well known today, but influential both locally and nationally at the time, was Buffalo architect William Worth Carlin. Carlin was very active in the Western Association of Architects (WAA) and the American Institute of Architects (AIA), two key and competing trade organizations for architects. Carlin played a pivotal role in the merger of the two groups in 1889. He successfully defeated Daniel Burnham for the WAA presidency in 1888, and Buffalo's Louise Bethune served as Carlin's second vice-president. Carlin was also president of the New York State architect's association and vice president of the merged AIA/WAA under Richard Morris Hunt. He helped to standardize contracts and fee rates used nationally.

None of Carlin's Buffalo buildings are known to have survived, but many of those by his partner and protege John Coxhead have. Coxhead's best known local building is the Delaware Avenue Baptist Church (1894–1895), a Romanesque building with unique stained glass windows that would become somewhat of a Coxhead trademark. Coxhead's most famous buildings, unfortunately, are not in Buffalo. He designed the original ten campus buildings of Virginia Union University in Richmond, Virginia, all extant and listed on the National Register.

As noted above, Buffalo architect Louise Bethune was active in both the WAA and the AIA on a national and local basis. Generally acknowledged as the first professional female architect in the country, much of Bethune's work was commissioned through the firm she ran with her husband, Robert Bethune. The most notable extant building designed by Bethune is the 1904 Lafayette Square Hotel.

Although Buffalo's architects were among the most influential in the country at this time, this wasn't the only profession garnering Buffalo national attention.

Several trade journals of other industries were published in Buffalo during this time. These included the *Medical and Surgical Journal, United Workman, Lumberworld,* and *American Tanner.* By sharing with the world our lessons in these arenas, we continued to enhance our image.

AROUND TOWN

By 1900, although the 25 railroad lines coming into Buffalo had consolidated into just seven different companies, Buffalo was still the second largest railroad center in the country. Combined, these companies owned more than 3,500 acres in the city and had 20,000 employees, including their own police. They also owned most of the lake shipping companies and dominated the city's economy.

While this influenced the early part of the century, perhaps the most significant event during this time occurred on November 16, 1896. This was when the first alternating current was sent from the Adams power station in Niagara Falls to the Buffalo Street Railway Company, making it the first electric streetcar system in the United States. The next year, George Urban's Buffalo flour mill building purportedly was the first in the country to use totally electric motors for milling operations. With these electric motors, the mill ground roughly 1,200 barrels of flour per day. This easy and cheap supply of electricity, combined with the massive transportation facilities, kept Buffalo on the leading edge well into the 1950s.

Often forgotten in a review of Buffalo's industry is her stockyards. Originally built *c.* 1863 by the New York Central Railroad, Buffalo's primary stockyards were located along William Street. In 1892, a new Livestock Exchange building on William Street was designed by Louise Bethune. As the name implies, this building housed the livestock, primarily cattle, bought and sold in the city. It was located near the local slaughterhouses and meat packing plants and was an integral part of the overall stockyard area, which was nearly 100 acres in size. The associated meat packing industry claimed to be the largest east of Chicago and the fifth largest in the world.

After the end of the Spanish-American War, the country had a respite from international conflict. But that didn't mean that the government was ignoring possible threats. From 1898–1900, the government built the New 74th Regimental Armory, now known as the Connecticut Street Armory. Used today primarily for weddings, the expansive interior drill floor/ballroom area was one of the largest columnless halls in the world when built.

Buffalo also continued to build schools. Masten Park High School, designed by Milton Bebee, opened in 1897. On a site picked prior to 1900, Lafayette High School, designed by Esenwein and Johnson, became the third public high school in the city when it opened in 1903. In 1912, Masten Park would burn, and the new Masten Park High School was also designed by Esenwein and Johnson. Today, the building is now the City Honors High School.

While Buffalo residents were building wonderful commercial structures, churches and other religious buildings continued to dominate the Buffalo landscape in the late nineteenth century. By 1900, there were more than 200 churches of nearly two dozen denominations, several of them reflecting their ethnic origins.

The largest number of churches were Roman Catholic, with 56 congregations. This was more than double the second-place denomination of Baptist, with 27 churches. Methodist churches ranked a close third, with 26, while Episcopalian, Presbyterian, and Lutheran had 23, 22, and 21 respectively. The only denomination with churches numbering in the teens was the German Evangelical with 18. There were nine Jewish synagogues and seven German Evangelical Reformed. The Evangelical Fellowship had five churches and there were four each for the Congregationalists, Disciples, and United Presbyterians. There were three Free Baptist churches, two Unitarian, two Church of Christ, and one each of the Apostolic, Church of New Jerusalem, Greek Orthodox, Reform Church, Seventh Day Adventist, the United Brothers in Christ, and Universalist.

Buffalo's love affair with sports started during this time with the formation of a popular bicycle club, as well as the Country Club of Buffalo and an improved Buffalo Yacht Club.

The Buffalo Yacht Club was organized in 1860, making it the third such club in the country. It is the only international club, having another site at Port Albino in Canada. The club started running an annual regatta the year it was founded, a tradition that continues to the present. The first clubhouse building was built in 1864, but the one most identified with the club even today was built in 1893 during the city's glory years. Set at the foot of Porter Avenue, this picturesque clubhouse helped host Pan-American visitors as well as a variety of dignitaries over the years.

The Country Club of Buffalo was founded in 1889 and by 1894, the club had opened six holes on Branson Rumsey's farm near Delaware Park. The club lost its land to the Pan-American Exposition in 1899 and purchased 70 acres at the corner of Main and Bailey. For the Pan-Am, the original clubhouse was converted to the Woman's Pavilion, and the new clubhouse, designed by local architect George Cary, was built on the new grounds in 1901.

In 1910 the course was redesigned to meet championship standards by one of the country's most underrated golf course architects, Walter Travis. This improved course design won the club the honor of hosting the 1912 U.S. Open, which was won by John McDermott. The first U.S. Open was played in 1895 and just the year before the Buffalo match, McDermott had been the first American to win the match. The win in Buffalo made him the first American to win back to back U.S. Opens, a record he would keep until 1930. By then, the Country Club had moved again, to Williamsville, and the county had purchased the course. The county still runs it today as the Grover Cleveland Golf Course.

Yet while all this was happening, the most significant event to have a long-reaching impact on Buffalo and the nation occurred quietly in 1902. While working at Wendt's Buffalo Forge, Willis Carrier invented the air conditioner. His original invention was designed to help a New York City printer produce consistent prints that were not affected by the fluctuations in heat and humidity. Not understanding the potential applications at first, Carrier waited until 1906 to patent his invention. In 1915, he formed his own company, and started producing air conditioners for factories. The general public became aware of the advantages in the 1920s when theaters around the country started using air conditioners to attract customers in from their summer activities. And once the public got used to the cooler air, people demanded home applications. According to the Carrier Company history, by 1995, air conditioning was installed in more than 75 percent of homes in the United States.

Ironically, this single invention, when combined with other transportation and economic business conditions, would lead to Buffalo's decline in the late 1900s. But as we'll see, the intervening 50 years were among the most prosperous of times for the city.

Chapter Seven

PAN-AMERICAN ERA

In 1899, Buffalo began the preparations for one of its crowning moments of glory: the 1901 Pan-American Exposition. With $1.75 million raised by the Buffalo area and a $500,000 donation from Congress, Buffalo's leading citizens prepared to dazzle the world. The preparations for and grandeur of the exhibition, the death of President McKinley, and the years until 1910 are perhaps the most significant events in the city's history.

PLANNING FOR THE EVENT

While the specific planning for the Pan-American did not start until 1899, the city had, in fact, been preparing for the event for decades by hosting a number of smaller successful events. The first of these was the 1869 Mechanics Association's Industrial Exposition, designed to acquaint both Buffalonians and others in the Northeast with a variety of technologies.

This was followed in 1888 by the International Industrial Fair held in Hamlin Park. Similar to modern county and state fairs with races, concerts, and agricultural, art, and technology exhibits, this fair had an attendance of about 30,000 visitors per day. One of its big hits was the bicycle displays.

Another large event, held in 1897, was the Grand Army of the Republic (GAR) Convention. As Jacob Mueller states in his 1912 book, *Buffalo and Its German Community*:

> Because of its ideal location and ample supply of comfortable hotels
> Buffalo became one of the greatest and more beloved convention cities
> in America. As demonstrated by the hospitality offered August 23–28
> of 1897 with the "Encampment of the Grand Army of the Republic,"
> Buffalo proved that it was capable of handling large flocks of tourists.

More than 10,000 veterans camped for the week in the grounds near Fort Porter and an estimated 200,000 visited the city and GAR members during this time. The most famous visitor was President William McKinley, who arrived on August 24, attending a banquet that evening and participating in a parade the following day. An estimated 50,000 Civil War veterans marched in the parade. That evening, McKinley wandered among the various groups gathered at campfires and spoke with many of the men.

According to the *Journal of the 31st Encampment*, the Buffalo event was the largest in the organization's history and a success all around. "In point of weather, enthusiasm, the display of true comradeship on all sides, attendance, liberality, and thorough management on the part of Citizens' Committees, in fact everything . . ." was superb.

So Buffalo knew it could host large events. The city also knew what types of exhibits, buildings, and other attractions should be included in a world's fair. Respected Buffalonians had attended the International American Conference in Washington, D.C. in 1889, the Colombian Exposition in Chicago in 1893, and the Cotton States International Exposition in 1895, and were eager to show the world their thriving city. In 1898, then-mayor Conrad Diehl persuaded enough of the people to consider the idea that they were ready to form a committee. This committee sought government grants and public donations to support the fair. By early 1900, 11,000 people had pledged $1.5 million toward the fair and a site near Delaware Park, leased from the Rumsey's, was selected.

With $1.5 million raised by the Buffalo area, $200,000 from the state, a $500,000 donation from Congress, and $2.5 million in bonds, Buffalo's leading citizens prepared to dazzle the world. Since the first impressions of the fair would be its buildings, the first critical decision was on the overall layout of the grounds and the architectural style to use. Functioning as the advisory board of architects to the fair were a panel of the city's and the nation's leading architects: Chairman John M. Carrere of Carrere & Hastings in New York City; George Cary of Buffalo; Walter Cook of Babb, Cook and Willard in New York City; August C. Esenwein of Esenwein & Johnson in Buffalo; Edward B. Green of Green and Wicks in Buffalo; Robert S. Peabody of Peabody and Stearns in Boston; and George F. Shepley of Shepley, Routan & Coolidge in Boston. The architectural style chosen for the fair was Spanish Renaissance, honoring the dominant style of buildings in Central and South America.

But the plans for the buildings and grounds were only part of the complicated process. The various committees also had to solicit countries and states to provide exhibits, select food and other vendors, collect the appropriate speakers and other dignitaries needed to draw attendees, negotiate special discounts with hotels and railroads, hire workers, and perform a myriad of other duties. To try to minimize fire risk and subsequent damage, the committees also arranged for two hose companies, two engine companies, and one hook and ladder company and a chief to reside onsite for the six months of the show. Another safety measure was the on-grounds hospital, which would be put to a much more serious task than the planners ever imagined.

Anticipating the need for workers at the fair, day laborers descended on the city starting as early as March of 1901. It is estimated that over 300 people moved to Buffalo during the fair to work on the grounds as waiters, waitresses, bartenders, barkers, and the like.

An article in the April 13, 1901 issue of *The Outlook*, released just prior to the May 1 opening, included these kind words for the venue, "It will be held on the limits of one of the most beautiful cities in the country, and one especially adapted for the purposes of an Exposition; for there is no more comfortable summer city in America than Buffalo."

Since it was the largest national event following the successful conclusion of the Spanish-American War, everyone, it seemed, looked forward to the opening of the exposition.

OPENING CELEBRATIONS

By 1901, as the promotional literature boasted, the city had 2 libraries, 60 public schools, 187 churches, 9 theaters, and 24 banks and trusts, as well as its 300 miles of paved roads and 1,000 acres of parks. In addition to the amenities listed above, Buffalo at that time had 28 railroad lines and continued lake and canal shipping ventures, making it the world's largest grain port, largest lumber port, second largest cattle market, and sixth largest overall port. So boast the city could to the more than 8 million people who would journey to the Pan-American that year.

The planning for the fair had included an extensive opening ceremony for opening day, May 1, 1901. To a standing room only crowd, headed by the appropriate dignitaries from the various countries and states, including U.S. Vice-President Teddy Roosevelt, the exhibition president John Milburn read an opening message from President McKinley. This was followed by some musical selections and then speeches by Vice-President Roosevelt and New York's Governor Woodruff.

Once the opening festivities were over, the crowds were ready to explore the buildings and grounds. The overall layout of the exhibition was cruciform, with wide courtyards and mall-like areas between the various buildings. The primary open space was in the center of the exposition, with the Esplanade running east/west and a series of courts and walkways running north/south. The southernmost court, called Fore Court, was accessed via the "Approach." Heading north from this court, attendees passed across the Triumphal Bridge over the east and west portions of Mirror Lake and then into the Esplanade. Leaving the Esplanade again to the north was the Fountain of Abundance, then the Court of Fountains, to the magnificent Electric Tower, and finally on to the Plaza and Propylaea. On the northeast corner of this major traffic area were the stadium and most of the agricultural-related displays. Designed to hold 12,000 people, the stadium actually packed in 15,000 for the more popular events.

On the southeast of the courts were the exhibitions and displays of all the states and foreign countries, with the exception of the New York State building, which was on the southwest side with the gardens and the Woman's Building. The major technology buildings and the Midway were in the central and northwest sections.

As the name Mirror Lake implied, the major display buildings on the east and west largely mirrored one another. South to north, these pairs included the Horticulture and United States Government buildings, the Temple of Music and Ethnology buildings, the Machinery and Transportation and the Manufacturers and Liberal Arts buildings, and the Electricity and Agricultural buildings.

At most major exhibitions, the buildings are intended to be temporary, and this was true with the Pan-American, too. The buildings were constructed of plaster over wire rather than with traditional wood or masonry. The only exception to this was the New York State Building, which was built of marble, and was designed to become the new home of the Buffalo Historical Society. Still overlooking one of the ponds on the edge of Delaware Park, the Historical Society Building (designed by local architect George Cary) gives us a sense of what the other buildings were like.

Though not housed in permanent buildings, other states represented at the Pan-American included the New England states in the New England Building, Pennsylvania, Minnesota, Illinois, and Ohio. Foreign countries included Cuba and Chile. A visitor to these state pavilions during the exhibition commented that one of the most interesting things about each state building was the visitor logs. Since each state asked for registration information including name, place of birth, and current address, reading through the logs allowed old acquaintances to look one another up after they returned home from the fair.

Quite a few of the exhibits at the fair were designed to highlight life in the Americas, both present and past, while others were designed to display American ingenuity, and still others were just for fun. One of the lifestyle exhibits was designed to show what life on the prairie was like in the late nineteenth century. It included a real sod house, brought in from Nebraska and set up as it would have been in 1884. The exhibit also included a log cabin, adobe house, and a primitive native house.

Several of the state exhibits also included lifestyle-related areas, primarily representing exported products. Florida and California had displays of oranges and grapefruit, South Carolina had one of tea, and the Puerto Rico exhibit included a coffee plantation display. Other states highlighted the more typical agriculture products such as wheat, corn, and the like, running the gamut from grains to vegetables to fruits. Another popular exhibit was sponsored by the federal government. It had wax models of United States military people in the appropriate uniforms of the various branches and time periods.

Other "slice of life" displays had much more serious connotations. One such exhibit was the charity-sponsored tenement exhibit. With models of the deplorable conditions of tenements in New York City and a model of the new tenement under the 1901 tenement law, this display highlighted the need for new housing laws in other major cities, too. In addition to the models for New York, there were photographs showing examples of the differences between the typical and the worst housing in Buffalo and Albany; as well as the major Ohio cities, Cleveland, Cincinnati, and Dayton; the Pennsylvania cities of Philadelphia and Pittsburgh; St. Paul Minnesota; Washington, D.C.; Detroit, Michigan; and Chicago, Illinois.

Another serious exhibit that may or may not have been taken seriously at the time was the American Negro Exhibit. Placed in the Pan-American to counter the somewhat negative "Darkest Africa" and "The Old Plantation" exhibits, this exhibit focused on the many contributions of African Americans to their new country. A reincarnated version of the popular exhibit at the 1900 Paris Exposition, this showed photographs of leading African-American colleges and their graduates, gave population statistics, and listed books and patents by African Americans.

Foreign Midway exhibits with local ethnic connections were special attractions. One of these was called "Alt Nurnberg" which meant "Old Nuremberg," named after a city in the southeast area of Germany. While the exhibit did include replicas of some of the more historic Nuremberg buildings, the primary attraction was the German restaurant, providing meals to weary visitors. The Italian "Venice in America" was also popular. Tourists could take gondola rides around the exhibition canal and be serenaded by mandolins as if they were really in Italy.

One of the most unexpected yet interesting "exhibits" at the fair was the Infant Incubator Building. Located near the West Amherst entrance gate where the Mall crossed the Midway, the display showed how incubators could save the lives of an additional 60 percent of premature babies. Although incubators had been invented around 1840, they were not readily used yet by 1901. The infants in the incubators were real babies from Buffalo families, and just like the specimens in a zoo, each sported a ribbon to tell visitors the baby's sex and a placard giving height, weight, and other data to explain why the baby was in the incubator.

Other medical technology being pumped was x-ray technology. Originally invented in 1896, by 1901, x-rays were still not in common use. The Pan-American x-ray exhibit in the Science Hall was designed to show how beneficial x-rays could be, especially in surgical procedures. That would prove to be an especially ironic coincidence later in the year.

Another relatively new technology on display was a switchboard from the Kellogg Telephone Company. Claiming to be the largest switchboard of its time, the massive piece of equipment could accommodate 12,000 individual lines in sections of 300 lines each. Built of a solid mahogany front, glass side panels, and a curtained rear access, its main advantage was in the simplified design of the jacks, which hid the major wiring on the back of the board. In other words, it was built for show as well as function.

The highlight of the fair were the evening light shows, powered by the new Niagara Falls electric plant. Each building was trimmed with electric bulbs, and when darkness descended, some 500,000 of these specially designed bulbs brought the fair to new life. Especially beautiful at night was the Electric Tower, the tallest structure at the fair. What differentiated this lighting, and the overall appearance of this fair from the 1893 Chicago Fair, was its emphasis on color. Unlike the stark white of the Columbian Exposition, vibrant color dominated the buildings at the Pan-American Exposition.

In his 1901 *National Magazine* article on the fair, Joe Mitchell Chapple proclaims, "The outlines of the buildings traced in the rows of electric lights; the softening colors and brilliant play of glass and gilding, and the reflection of this fairy land in the surrounding waters; the jewelled spray of cascade and fountains, and the almost spiritual beauty of group and statue, form a picture that can never be forgotten."

Lillian Betts in her "The People at the Pan-American" essay in *The Outlook* is as poetic:

> The few lights on the posts have disappeared, and semi-darkness envelops the scene. Pink dots appear everywhere. The Tower is softly luminous, the light coming from within; arches, domes, roofs, windows, columns, capitals, statues, are outlined by those pink dots of light. Softly but clearly the notes of the "Star-Spangled Banner" float on the air. The people sitting rise, hats are removed; here and there a head is bowed; one feels the thrill of thousands of hearts moved by one great emotion. The dots of pink have now become lines of soft radiance growing whiter each minute. Strong and full are the notes of a song that, under the influence of the time, is a nation's anthem. So perfectly timed is this wonder of light that its fullest radiance is reached as the last note of music dies away.

This combination of light and patriotic song must have been magnificent, but it wasn't just the buildings and exhibits that were attractions. The diversity in social status, clothing, language, accents within the same language, ages, hair color, hair style, and demeanor of attendees was so striking that many of the visitors to the fair commented that watching the other visitors was also entertaining.

But not all the effects of the exposition were positive, especially to the residents. Tacky temporary restaurants and stores sprang up all along Main Street as well as near the exhibition gates. Not only were these places unsightly, they served highly discounted food and beverages in the hopes of making a quick buck on products of questionable quality. The established businesses, on the other hand, raised their prices. During the summer of 1901, the prices at soda fountains doubled. While this was good for the local business people, the residents had to contend with crowded conditions as well as the increased expense.

BUFFALO'S BLEAKEST HOUR

Unfortunately, the fair is most frequently remembered not for its magnificent setting, buildings, and venue, but for the untimely death of President William McKinley. President McKinley was fatally wounded while presiding over a public reception in the Temple of Music on September 6, 1901. He died eight days later.

BUFFALO

McKinley enjoyed fairs and he enjoyed Buffalo, having been to the city during the 1897 GAR convention as well as on other occasions. He had intended to be at the Pan-American opening ceremonies on May 1, but was unable to come because his wife became ill. He was greatly disappointed, especially as Roosevelt and others who had been to the fair proclaimed its wonders.

Determined not to miss the entire fair, McKinley and the exhibition committee rearranged some events and made September 5 President's Day. McKinley, his wife, and the rest of his entourage arrived in Buffalo on the evening of September 4 on a special train that proceeded directly to the fair grounds. After a brief tour of the grounds, the party retired to the Milburn house, where they were staying.

The following morning the President gave a rousing speech and spent the day touring the fair. On the morning of September 6, the President went to visit Niagara Falls and the new power plant, then returned to Buffalo for the final afternoon reception. A crowd had been gathering outside the Temple of Music for several hours before the doors opened. Once inside, the people queued to meet the President, who was standing at the front of the hall with Milburn and others. It was common in those days for people to carry handkerchiefs, for their traditional purpose as well as to wipe sweaty brows, so no one thought anything was amiss when Leon Czolgosz approached the President with a handkerchief in his hand. Unfortunately, Czolgosz was concealing a pistol and shot McKinley twice in the stomach.

Czolgosz was not from Buffalo, but from Detroit, and had come to town specifically to try to kill the President. After the shooting, he was brought down by others in the crowd and detained as McKinley was quickly taken to the exhibition hospital. This was one of the first mistakes made in the handling of the shooting. The next was in the selection of the primary physician. Since Roswell Park, the city's leading surgeon, was unavailable, an obstetrician, Dr. Mann, with little surgical knowhow, was selected to evaluate the President's condition. He determined that an immediate operation was required. Due to the lateness of the hour, though, there was insufficient light in the makeshift operating room to properly remove the bullets. The attendants were forced to maximize the remaining sunshine with mirrors to try to get enough light.

Mann found that one bullet had not penetrated the skin, but he could not locate the second. He could tell that it had not ruptured any of the critical internal organs, so he decided to close the incisions just about as the attendants managed to get an electric light installed. Rather then going back in and verifying his assumptions, Mann proceeded to finish closing.

As news spread of the incident, mobs gathered both at the fair and then later at the police station where Czolgosz was being held. The National Guard was called in to help control the crowd, and McKinley was moved from the fairgrounds to the Milburn house to recuperate.

Initial reports were positive, and the city and the country were led to believe that the President was recovering and would be fine in due time. Vice-President Roosevelt, who had been called to Buffalo after the shooting, was so convinced, he left Buffalo for a hiking trip in the Adirondacks. But, in fact, the President was weakening daily. Seeing his condition, McKinley's private secretary had arranged to have Thomas Edison send his latest x-ray machine to Buffalo so that the doctors could find the bullet still lodged in the President's abdomen. Yet the doctors refused to use it. This allowed gangrene to set in and eventually infect the major internal organs.

On September 13 at 5:00 p.m., McKinley had a heart attack, and at 8:00 he said his goodbyes to his wife. He went into a coma at 9:00 and died shortly after 2:00 a.m. the following morning.

After a frantic manhunt for Roosevelt, he was notified of the President's real condition, and returned by private train. The morning of McKinley's death, after a brief swearing-in ceremony at the Ansley Wilcox house, Roosevelt became President. A modest wake was held in Milburn's house where the President had died and then McKinley's body was taken to City Hall, where thousands of mourners paid their last respects. McKinley was then buried in his hometown, Canton, Ohio.

And once the President died, so did the Pan-American Exposition. Although the exhibition remained open until its original ending date of November 1, attendance at the fair dropped precipitously after the assassination. The people who had come to town returned home, and those who had intended to come cancelled their plans.

Meanwhile, Czolgosz's trial took place, starting on September 23 and lasting a brief three days. He was found guilty of murder and sentenced to death. He was executed in the Auburn State Penitentiary on October 29, just two days before the official ending of the exhibition.

In 1907, a monument to McKinley designed by New York architects Carrere and Hastings was placed in Niagara Square. Daniel Burnham is said to have suggested the obelisk shape and chosen the Niagara Square location.

BUFFALO

Aftermath

Press reports just after the closing of the Pan-American state that the exhibition lost between $3 million and $6 million. On the other hand, Kenneth W. Luckhurst, in his 1951 book, *The Story of Exhibitions*, gives the following figures: Expenses, $9,447,750; Gate/Income: $8,869,750. These numbers show a difference of less than $600,000.

Buffalonians tend to point to the fact that the Pan-American lost money as proof that the fair was not a success, but most of the large fairs held from 1850 through 1950, in fact, lost money. The only three that made any money at all were the 1867 Paris Fair, the 1876 Philadelphia Centennial, and the 1893 Columbian Exhibition. But these three received heavy subsidies from the respective federal governments, far exceeding the $700,000 given to the Pan-American by New York and the United States.

Compared to other large exhibitions, the Pan-American actually fared quite well. If the Luckhurst figures are correct and the organizers lost approximately $600,000, this is a net deficit of only six percent of the total expenses. The next major United States fair in St. Louis in 1904, on the other hand, lost more than $5 million, totaling 19 percent of the expenses. And the citizens of St. Louis had to make up this huge deficit. Even if the actual Pan-American loss was in the $3–6 million range, the 1939 New York World's Fair lost more than twice that much.

Organizers of other similar fairs had in fact predicted that the Pan-American would lose money for the city. "Will the Pan-American Fair Be a Bad Thing for Buffalo?" in the June 8, 1901 issue of *Literary Digest* discussed this very topic. It quotes a *Chicago Tribune* article as saying the exposition:

> reflects credit on the energy, artistic taste, and liberality of the citizens of Buffalo. . . . It does not reflect equal credit on their powers of observation and their business sense. For an exposition is a speculation which never pays the city where it may be held, however much it may benefit those who attend it. For that city it means a few months of feverish excitement and jubilation, and then a reaction and long-continued deadly dulness. A year hence the Buffalonians who are up in a balloon now will be down on the ground, meditating on the unprofitableness of expositions.

This is precisely what the Buffalo organizers found. Even without the rainy spring weather, which lowered attendance in May and June, and even without the horror of losing President McKinley, it is likely the exhibition would have lost money.

So while the Pan-American did lose money, this really can't be used as the sole determinant of success. Much more important is the fact that attendance at the fair topped 8 million in just four months (since the final two months really don't count). The fair managed to showcase the technological innovations for which it was designed and highlighted the city and its wonderful achievements. This is what should be remembered most about the Pan-American Exposition.

Chapter Eight

WORLD WAR I ERA

By 1910, of the 12,000 Buffalo workers in steel-related industries, Lackawanna Steel employed 60 percent. The plant continued to grow into the 1920s. World War I era Buffalo also saw growth in the budding aviation industry. Glenn Curtiss, an airplane inventor, opened a large plant in 1915. By 1918, Curtiss had expanded to more than 120,000 square feet of plants in the area and employed 18,000 workers.

PRELUDE TO WAR

Although Buffalonians lost some of their heart after the Pan-American, many companies continued to thrive. By 1910, the population of Buffalo had expanded again to 423,715. All the associated infrastructure also increased and improved. In 1911, the fire companies first used motor vehicles as cars for the chief and his assistant, and then in 1912, the first motorized pumper was put in service.

There were 62,227 children attending the 62 public schools by 1911, including 3,850 at the high schools already mentioned and another 515 at the new technical high school. By 1912, there were also approximately 7,500 students attending church-run schools in 17 parishes. Between 1921 and 1925, eight more public grade schools and one high school, Bennett High, were constructed.

Several of the city's most prominent buildings were erected during this time, changing the city's skyline both in profile and in height. The average building height at the turn of the century was 52 feet, and by 1920, it had grown to 112 feet. Taller minor buildings influenced this change, as did the building of some giant structures.

The most notable of the tall structures in this era is the General Electric Building, now known as the Niagara Mohawk Building. Designed by local architects Esenwein and Johnson, the building opened in 1912. With its white terra cotta over the reinforced concrete and steel of the 300 foot octagonal central tower, it is still one of the most prominent buildings in the city. This is especially true at night, when the tower is lit with red, white, and blue spotlights, making it the perfect place for the annual Buffalo New Year's Eve festivities.

BUFFALO

Two other major office buildings—the Liberty National Bank Building and the Rand Building—added their height to the skyline post–World War I. The Liberty National Bank, formerly the German-American Bank, built its new headquarters at the southwest corner of Main and Court in 1925. The twin replicas of the Statue of Liberty that are perched atop each tower face east and west, symbolizing Buffalo's importance in connecting those two sections of the country. The Rand Building, built in 1929, is opposite the Liberty Building, on the northeast corner of Main and Lafayette Square.

New churches continued to be built as congregations outgrew their old buildings. One of the city's largest churches of this time opened in 1912. Founded in 1817, the Riverside Methodist Episcopal Church worshiped in a facility at Bird and West Avenue from 1872 until 1912. The congregation built its new church on the corner of Baynes and Potomac.

Religious-related charitable organizations also evolved and matured exponentially before the war. The largest of these was the YMCA, which grew from a single branch in 1852 to eight by 1909. The largest branch was located at the intersection of Mohawk, Genesee, and Franklin Streets. Designed in 1901 by Green and Wicks, the ten-story building has two four-story wings on each side following the contours of the irregularly shaped lot. Opened in 1902, it originally had 1,800 rooms.

In the retail arena, some dominant players of the era included James Noble Adam and his brother Robert B. Adam. The former was the founder of the J.N. Adam department store, and the latter a founder of the Adam, Meldrum and Anderson (AM&As) department store. J.N. Adam founded his store in 1881, but his brother's store was first. Robert Adam and Alexander Meldrum opened their first store in 1867. When William Anderson joined the firm in 1875, the store took on its well-recognized name.

Together, the Adam brothers would dominate the retail industry in Buffalo for decades. J.N. Adam went on to serve as mayor of Buffalo from 1906 to 1909 and was also chiefly responsible for Buffalo's first tuberculosis hospital in Perrysburg, New York. Adam donated the land on which the hospital sits and it was named the J.N. Adam Tuberculosis Hospital in his honor. The original hospital buildings were designed by Buffalo's John Coxhead and opened in 1912.

Another major player in the Buffalo retail scene at this time was Seymour Knox. Founder of the S.H. Knox Five and Dime, which later merged with F.W. Woolworth, Knox built two mansions on Delaware Avenue and a large estate in East Aurora. He also sat on the board of numerous philanthropical groups and was an active member in the Delaware Avenue Baptist Church.

World War I Era

The leading medical personality in Buffalo during this time was surgeon and teacher Roswell Park. Park, a ninth-generation American, moved to Buffalo from Chicago in 1883 to teach surgery at the university medical school. He was lured from his adopted Chicago by the promise he saw in the evolving city, which he had first become familiar with when he attended the 1878 American Medical Association conference held here. Thirty-one at the time, he was already considered one of the premiere doctors in the country.

Over the next 30 years, Park would become increasingly popular both in the city and in the nation. In 1892, when a Chicago job offer threatened to draw Park away, the Goodyear brothers, Albright, and other leading businessmen persuaded him to stay by funding the building of a new medical school, opened in 1893. But Park didn't focus just on his medical program. He lobbied strongly for the broadening of the university degree programs, and the American Medical Association (AMA) agreed with him. They mandated at least a year of liberal arts education in addition to medical studies, and in 1913, to meet the AMA requirement, Park was finally rewarded with the university's introduction of a liberal arts curriculum. This later evolved into a full-fledged liberal arts degree program, altering the future of the university.

When the city hosted the Pan-American Exposition, it was Park who was put in charge of all the health-related aspects. He regretted until his own death being unavailable to operate on McKinley after the shooting.

In addition to his practice at the hospital and his teaching at the university, Park was a prolific author. He wrote more than 150 articles and a variety of books during his career. In 1897 his book on the history of medicine was released and in 1905 he published a seminal work on brain surgery.

Despite his interest in many surgical topics, his love was for cancer research. He avidly studied tumors and believed that the cancer rate was increasing and needed to be thoroughly studied. He convinced the university to open a cancer research facility called the Gratwick Laboratory. In 1911, New York State took over the funding of the center, renaming it the New York State Laboratory and Hospital for the Study of Malignant Diseases. Thus was established the first cancer research center in the country.

Because of the nature of his work, Park often contracted diseases from his patients, and over time, this repeated assault on his health was too great to bear. He died in 1914 of heart failure at the age of 62. But his legacy lives on in today's Roswell Park Cancer Institute, still one of the leading cancer facilities in the world.

BUFFALO

But prominent citizens were not the only ones making lives for themselves in the City of Good Neighbors. Throughout the early 1900s, arriving immigrants continued to settle in the lower East Side until they could afford to move out. This started to change in the 1920s as thousands of African Americans settled in this area. By 1930, there were more than 13,000 African Americans in the city and they had developed their own infrastructure. There were hotels, clubs, funeral homes, markets, a church, a theater, and a YMCA in the area, making it a city within a city. Even with this increase in population, Germans were still the largest immigrant group with 38 percent of the population.

In 1925, two important transportation-related events took place. After serving the city for 100 years, the last remnants of the Erie Canal were turned into a four lane road. This closed one era of transportation as a new one emerged with the opening of the Buffalo Municipal Airport in Cheektowaga. This new airport predates those in most of the other major U.S. cities.

Despite the closing of the canal, business in Buffalo was still booming. The port was still the largest in the world in the grain industry and second largest in milling. Other industries were also blossoming. By 1910, Buffalo had more than 1,500 manufacturing companies employing nearly 70,000 people. There were 18 banks and trust companies. Buffalo's Lackawanna coal trestle, nearly 1 mile in length, was the largest in the world.

And railroads, especially the New York Central, were key. In 1926, New York Central decided to build a new terminal east of downtown. Completed in 1928, Central Terminal was one of the finest Art Deco buildings in the country. It was the largest station that New York Central owned and could house in the office tower nearly 2,000 employees. The main lobby was 225 feet in length, 66 feet in width, and crowned by 59-foot domes at each end. With its 15-story central tower and 450-foot concourse, the immense building was also designed to impress arriving passengers with Buffalo's grandeur. The gold-toned Buffalo statue in the terminal was a favorite meeting place for travelers arriving and departing on the approximately 200 passenger trains traveling in and out on the 14 different tracks.

Another major project completed during this time was the Peace Bridge between Buffalo and Fort Erie, Canada. Opened in 1927, the bridge is still Buffalo's main access point to and from Canada. Even though not implemented until the 1920s, the bridge was not a twentieth-century idea. The idea was actually raised as early as 1851. But serious impediments, such as appropriate legislation on the part of both countries, funding issues, opposing groups, and the nature of the river currents themselves, kept the project on the back burner for decades.

In 1893, Alonzo Mather developed the first concrete plans for a bridge, but since his idea included an additional power station, the power giants in Niagara Falls quashed the idea.

But this had whetted people's appetites for a bridge. The idea surfaced again in 1909 when forward looking citizens in both countries decided a span decorated with monuments reflecting both countries would be an appropriate way to celebrate the fast approaching century of peace between the two nations. The idea continued to spread when 40,000 people attended a peace rally of celebration in 1913.

At the end of World War I, interest was renewed. Three Buffalo businessmen convinced the United States to form a bridge commission and the group was incorporated in New York State in 1919. Their Canadian colleagues were able to do the same thing in Canadian government. By 1925, legislation allowing the building of a bridge was finally passed in each country, a single bridge company was formed, and it proceeded to purchase the land on which to anchor the bridge. Nearly $5 million was raised through the issuing of bonds, with the first $3 million selling in approximately 20 minutes.

Construction started in August of 1925, and less than two years later, the span was opened. The opening was attended by the Prince of Wales and the governor of New York, as well as the British and Canadian prime ministers and the U.S. vice president and secretary of state.

As noted earlier, a wide variety of industries were operating in Buffalo prior to and during the war. Despite this, there were three industries that dominated the city—automotive, aviation, and steel.

CARS, CARS, EVERYWHERE

The automobile was first introduced around 1885 in Germany by Karl Benz. Credited as the first American automobile manufacturers are the Duryea Brothers in 1892. In their early days, cars were popular among the wealthy but weren't popular with the general public because of the relatively high cost. This didn't stop adventuresome entrepreneurs from trying to get into the market, however. While automobile companies sprang up all over the United States, a great number of them were located in Buffalo. The first automobile in the city appeared around 1895 and by the early 1900s, Buffalo had more than 30 car manufacturers employing more than 15,000 people.

One of the most popular Buffalo automobile companies during this time was the Pierce-Arrow Motor Company. Born in Pennsylvania in 1846, George Pierce had moved to Buffalo in 1863. He worked at a variety of jobs until 1873 when he joined the Gesellgen, Heinz & Company organization. Founded in 1865, the company produced disparate household products including birdcages and iceboxes. When Pierce joined the company, he was made a partner and the name was changed to the Heinz, Pierce and Munshauer Company. Pierce left the firm in 1878 to form George N. Pierce & Company. His new company produced similar household products, but the product that brought attention to the firm was not introduced until nearly ten years later, when it is said the company introduced its first tricycle.

The following year, 1889, the company introduced its first adult bike, which went on to be very popular among the nation's cyclists. Even the bicycle-based police force during the Pan-American tooled around on Pierce's bikes, made in Pierce's factory on Hanover Street.

In 1900, Pierce jumped on the automobile bandwagon, first with a steam engine and then in 1901 with a gas engine. This 1901 2-horsepower "horseless carriage" was called the Motorette, and Pierce debuted it at the Pan-American by driving it around the exhibition grounds on opening day. He caused quite a stir, and in the next two years, produced around 150 cars selling at $950 each.

Within five years, Pierce's company had grown so large that it needed a new facility. In 1904, the first models called Pierce-Arrow were produced, and by 1906, Pierce had selected a site on Elmwood that had been a part of the Pan-American for his larger factory. He chose Albert Kahn as architect to design a well-lighted, open configuration facility. Kahn delivered the factory in 1906, and it proved to be a model for large manufacturing facilities throughout the next several decades. Ford, Martin (aerospace), and Buffalo-based Curtiss-Wright used Kahn in the next decades to design their factories. A new administration building for the factory was also built and this was designed by local architect George Cary. The complex at 1695 Elmwood Avenue is listed on the National Register of Historic Places.

The new factory originally had about 9 acres of floor space, but even that was not enough for the booming company. By 1912, the company had expanded into 12 buildings with a total of 23 acres of shop floor rambling over 15 acres of the city. Nearly 4,000 people were employed there in 1912 and at its peak, it is said that more than 10,000 people worked there.

Part of what spurred the growth of the company was how well the cars did in competitions. In a new competition called the Glidden Tour, held in July 1905, Pierce's son Perry won with a four-cylinder model called the Great Arrow. The company continued to win the next four competitions.

World War I Era

In 1907, the corporate name was changed to the Pierce-Arrow Motor Car Company to reflect the new focus on motorized vehicles. Although George Pierce retired that same year, the company continued to garner several first and largest distinctions in the automotive industry. One of the most important of these "firsts" occurred in 1909 when President William Taft, in 1909, became the first President to requisition presidential automobiles. He purchased two models of Pierce-Arrow cars, the Landaulette and the Brougham. For the next 26 years, even through Roosevelt and the Depression, each President would get a Pierce-Arrow car for himself.

The year 1914 heralded two firsts. The Pierce-Arrow 66 debuted, sporting an 824-cubic inch, 12-cylinder engine. To this day, it is the largest production model car engine ever produced. The other 1914 first was a new fender-based pair of headlights. Although the more traditional style headlights were kept available through 1932, most Pierce-Arrow cars were built with the patented fender style lights, which became a Pierce-Arrow trademark.

During World War I, Pierce-Arrow built a line of trucks, too. These 2-ton and 5-ton trucks were popular with the American Allies, France, and England, so much so that throughout the war years, Pierce-Arrow built many more trucks than it did cars. In 1911, it produced approximately 2,000 cars and did not reach those numbers again until 1919.

Pierce introduced the Series 33 car in 1921 and it continued to be the company's leading product through 1926. Ironically, production peaked in 1929 with nearly 8,500 cars. That same year, the company opened a wonderful Art Deco showroom at 2421 Main Street, several blocks north from the previous showroom at 752–758 Main.

From 1931 to 1933, automobile visionary Preston Tucker worked as plant manager in the Buffalo Pierce-Arrow plant. He went on to invent many of the safety features we know today, including them in the design of his infamous Tucker car in the late 1940s. While Tucker's car promised to revolutionize the automotive industry, it was quashed by his competition.

One of the more unique Pierce-Arrow products was introduced in 1936: the Travelodge trailer. Made of an aluminum shell and a steel body, the trailer was purportedly as luxurious as the Pierce-Arrow cars. Just as do modern trailers, it contained sleeping and dining areas, a gas cook stove, an icebox, and a water tank. It had a separate wood stove for heat on cool nights, and the walls were a mix of birch and gumwood. In the next two years, more than 400 Travelodge trailers were built.

Unfortunately for Pierce-Arrow, the quality of the cars it was producing made them too expensive for the masses and the Depression took its toll on the rich.

In 1928, Pierce-Arrow merged with Studebaker, although they each continued to produce their own line of cars. By 1933, Studebaker went bankrupt. Several Buffalo businessmen bought the Pierce-Arrow assets, but could not manage to keep the company afloat. In 1938, with only 26 cars produced, the company closed its doors.

The other world-renowned car manufacturer based in Buffalo was the E.R. Thomas Motor Car Company. Founded in 1902 by Erwin Thomas, this company, too, started as a bicycle manufacturer. In 1896 Thomas added a motor to one of his bike models and marketed it as the "Auto-Bi." In 1899 he designed a four-wheeled car with a one-cylinder engine and began selling it. In 1905 the cars started being referred to as Thomas Flyers, and the most famous was the 1907 model, which won the 1908 New York to Paris Race. With just some spare tires, additional gas tanks and other minor enhancements, the stock Flyer covered the 12,000-plus land miles in 170 days. Sales increased after the race and in 1911, the company introduced a six-cylinder model. By the end of 1912, however, losses were too great and the company folded.

Another Buffalo company with automotive roots is the Tri-Continental Company, now known as Trico, formed in 1917 to produce windshield wipers. While driving in a rainstorm the previous year, the company's founder, John Oishei, had hit someone because he couldn't see him. This rattled Oishei and inspired him to develop his wiper device. Although there are several claims that Trico's wipers were the first, they apparently were not. Mary Anderson invented them in 1903 and holds a 1905 patent for wipers, 12 years prior to Oishei. But Trico's wipers were apparently the first to be used on the split slot windshields popular at that time, and Trico did grow to become the largest windshield wiper blade company in the world.

BUFFALO'S AVIATION GIANTS

Sometime before 1906, some members of the local bicycling clubs got together and founded the Aero Club of Buffalo. The oldest such club in the United States and the second oldest in the world, the club first drew local attention in 1906 when it brought a dirigible to town. Flying over the city for some two hours, it brought traffic to a standstill.

Building on the city's interest in flight, two world-renowned aviation-related companies would evolve in Buffalo during this time and continue to be of great importance through both world wars. The first was the Curtiss Aeroplane Company and the second was the Irving Air Chute Company.

Arriving in Buffalo in 1915, Glenn Curtiss leased the defunct Thomas Flyer plant on Niagara Street. Curtiss, who also got interested in airplanes from bicycling, was once known as "The Fastest Man on Earth" for setting a land speed record of 136 miles per hour on a motorcycle. In 1907, Curtiss teamed up with Alexander Graham Bell to design more efficient airplanes. In 1909, Curtiss won an aviation contest in Reims, France and became a target in a patent battle. Despite court battles with Orville and Wilbur Wright for patent infringement, Curtiss continued to design and manufacture planes in Hammondsport, New York.

By 1916, the Curtiss Aeroplane and Motor Company was contructing war planes for England and grew to be the world's largest aircraft manufacturer. By 1917, Curtiss built a new plant on Elmwood Avenue, which became the largest such facility in the world.

In 1929, the still dueling Curtiss and Wright companies merged into the Curtiss-Wright Corporation and built a new facility in Tonawanda. The company continued to produce military airplanes throughout the 1930s and until the end of World War II. At its peak, it employed nearly 20,000 workers. The plants closed in 1946 after the war ended the heavy demand for fighter planes.

The second aerospace company to move to Buffalo was the Irving Air Chute Company, founded by Leslie Irvin in 1919. Earlier that year, Irvin had designed and demonstrated the first "free fall" parachute harness and rip cords and got immediate military orders for the device. He decided to locate his plant in Buffalo and intended the company be called "Irvin Air Chute;" however, a typographical error during the incorporation process added the "g" to his last name. Rather than refile, Irvin kept the accidental company name.

Irvin was born in California in 1895 and by the time he was 19, he was working as a Hollywood stuntman. In 1914 he was first hired to do an aero stunt, and he had performed so many of these by 1918 that he decided he needed a safer parachute. That same year he experimented with new designs and in 1919 partnered with Air Force designer E.C. Hoffman to debut a chute in public at a McCook Field air show. By World War II, Irvin's company was the largest parachute company in the world. His flight jackets were also popular with pilots. The company continued to operate in Buffalo throughout the war.

LET THERE BE STEEL

Buffalo's harbor attracted not only new citizens, but enticed a major player in the steel industry to concentrate in Buffalo. Lackawanna Steel opened its first plant in the Buffalo area in 1901. By 1910, of the 12,000 Buffalo workers in steel-related industries, Lackawanna Steel employed 60 percent. The plant continued to grow into the 1920s.

Lackawanna Steel had been brought to Buffalo from Scranton, Pennsylvania by financier John Albright and other key Buffalonians including ex–Pan-American-president John Milburn and the Goodyear brothers. In anticipation of the deal, Albright had been buying up hundreds of acres of lakeshore land just south of the Buffalo city line since the turn of the century. At that time, the natural resources in Scranton were being depleted, and unions were asking for increased wages and benefits. This, combined with Buffalo's excellent port, convinced the company's management to relocate here.

By 1912, the Lackawanna Steel Company covered 1,500 acres and was considered one of the largest manufacturing facilities in the world. It had its own 4-mile long breakwater and private harbor. Total corporate employment was approximately 12,000, so the workforce in Buffalo represented more than half the company's total.

Although Lackawanna Steel was a major employer in the city, it is important to remember what early work conditions were like there. While the grain scoopers' work on the docks was back-breaking, it was not overtly dangerous. This was not the case in the steel factory. The heat was oppressive, the men had to work 12-hour shifts, seven days a week, and when it was time to rotate shifts, workers worked a full 24-hour day. This led to numerous accidents and injuries as well as an often discontented work force.

Bethlehem Steel purchased Lackawanna Steel in 1922 and throughout the rest of the decade spent $40 million renovating the plant, hoping to use the new facilities primarily for the developing car industry. The continual upgrade of equipment helped the company stay on the leading edge of the steel business into the 1970s.

During this time, Buffalo was also an important player in the brass and copper businesses, purported to be home to the largest manufacturers of copper and brass in the country, employing more than 2,000. All of these industries continued to thrive throughout World War II.

Chapter Nine

WORLD WAR II

Throughout the 1930s and 1940s, Buffalo's manufacturing plants continued to dominate employment in the city. Their success spurred the city, drawing thousands to live and work in Buffalo. This, combined with the influx of New Deal money, dramatically changed the city fabric yet again during this time. The prominent industries and people of the those times and Buffalo's contributions to the war effort shaped the mid-nineteenth century.

AROUND THE CITY

Both Buffalo's manufacturing capabilities and the supporting infrastructure continued to improve through the 1930s and 1940s, despite the Depression and World War II. A major influx of New Deal money in 1935 spurred development through 1937. A total of more than $45 million in federal money was used for improvements in public housing, a concert hall and auditorium, a stadium, new police and federal offices, a new sewer system, enhancements at the airport and the zoo, as well as the traditional funding for schools, streets, and the like.

With this money, the 14,000 seat Memorial Auditorium was built. The cornerstone for the building located at the southern end of Main Street was laid in 1939. Costing nearly $3 million, "The Aud" opened in 1940. It continued to be the primary indoor sports arena in town until 1996.

Construction on another public gathering place, the Roesch Memorial Stadium, was started in 1935. Also built with WPA funds, by the time the stadium opened in 1938, it was known as Civic Stadium. It was renamed War Memorial Stadium in 1960 for all those who served in the military during the various wars and conflicts. Locally, though, most people just called the stadium "The Old Rockpile." Located at Best and Masten, its aging character gained it a leading role in Robert Redford's 1984 classic, *The Natural*.

The third public building partially financed with federal funds was the 1938–1940 Kleinhans Music Hall. Named in honor of the wife of Edward Kleinhans, who donated $717,000 toward the project, the Kleinhans Music Hall was designed by master architects Eliel and Eero Saarinan. The interior acoustic design was provided by Charles Potwin. Still today it is one of the most acoustically perfect and best known music halls in the world.

In 1940, Buffalo produced three-quarters of the wall-board in the country. It was also home to Spencer-Kellogg, the country's largest linseed oil plant, and National Aniline, the largest dye plant in the country

While the major manufacturers in Buffalo were in the automotive, aerospace, and steel industries, there was actually a huge variety among the businesses. In fact, of the 339 United States manufacturing codes used for census-taking, Buffalo had at least one company falling into 200 different codes.

One of the most significant building projects during this time helped celebrate the city's centennial in high style: the new Buffalo City Hall. Started in 1929, the new City Hall building was completed in 1931 and dedicated on Independence Day 1932. Designed by local architects Dietel and Wade, this Art Deco building is even more magnificent than Central Terminal. Placed directly over Court Street in Niagara Square, the 32-story building has beautiful figures, friezes, and tile work to tell the story of Buffalo.

Even in the depths of the Depression, the building cost nearly $7 million. It is just under 400 feet high, with office space in 26 of the floors totalling approximately 300,000 square feet. One of the most intriguing design features in the building was the use of passive air conditioning. Wind off the lake was funneled through large intake vents into the ground under the basement, then back through central cooling vents. Also humorous is the fact that each of the seats in the council chambers has its own hat rack.

The population in 1940 was over 575,000, and the city was still a major railroad hub, with ten railroad lines and three major train stations. The New York Central Railroad, the Michigan Central, the Pennsylvania, and the Toronto, Hamilton and Buffalo Railroads stop in Buffalo at Central Terminal. The Delaware, Lackawanna & Western, Baltimore and Ohio, and New York, Chicago and St. Louis Railroads stopped at the Lackawanna station. The Lehigh Valley, Erie, and Canadian National Railroads stopped at the Lehigh Valley Station.

In addition to the trains, business and social visitors could arrive and depart by bus, boat, and airplane. Thirteen different bus lines stopped at three different bus stations; four boat lines docked in the harbor; and the airport was serviced by two airlines, American and Pennsylvania Central.

To provide lodging for these travelers, the city had 76 hotels and tourist homes. For entertainment there were 6 radio stations, 2 theaters for "legitimate stage plays" and 67 movie theaters, 4 golf courses, 66 tennis courts, and 4 public swimming pools.

Sports continued to be important to the city and surrounding areas, before, during, and after the war. One of the most exciting events was the return to Buffalo of a championship golf tournament. The PGA Championship Tournament, first played in 1916, came to the area in 1934, to the Park Country Club in Williamsville. Won by Paul Runyan, this was, unfortunately, the last "major" golf event held in the area.

Professional baseball's tenure in the city fared much better. The Buffalo Bisons, founded in 1879, had been providing the city with a half-century of baseball by 1930. Starting in 1886 and continuing for nearly 40 years, the team played in the former Olympic Park, at Summer and Richmond. And in 1886, the Bisons also acquired their star batter, Frank Grant, considered by many to be the greatest African-American player in the nineteenth century. Grant was the home run king of the league the following year, but by the following year, anti-black sentiment in the league drove him out of Buffalo and out of professional baseball.

A new Olympic Park was built in 1889 at Michigan and Ferry and the Bisons moved there. In 1923, the Bisons played in the half demolished old stadium and prepared for the 1924 opening of the new 13,000-seat "Bison Stadium," later renamed the Offermann Stadium. Although that first season in the new stadium was disappointing, the team rallied in 1927, earning the pennant by winning an astounding 67 percent of their games with a team some credit as the best in the franchise's history.

They increased their presence with several other stellar seasons during the 1930s and 1940s. In 1936, the Bisons won 61 percent of their games, including a streak of 14, winning them the pennant again, this time over Rochester. They placed in the top five many times over the next decade, and then as the 1940s drew to a close, struck gold once more, winning the pennant with a 58 percent win season.

The ethnic and racial tension felt by Buffalo's black baseball players in the late 1800s became generalized among all of Buffalo's residents throughout the early twentieth century. The residential areas of the city had divided by nationality, ethnicity, and social status by 1940, with the wealthiest living along Delaware Avenue and its major side streets and parallel streets. Approximately 20 percent of the city was Polish and lived in Little Poland, on the east side of Main Street. For the first time, the Germans in Buffalo were the second largest nationality, many of whom lived in the German East Side, but many also had integrated with the other residents throughout the city. The third largest ethnic group was Italian, with 80,000 people, clustered primarily along the waterfront. Hungarians were by then a large part of the city, too, with 15,000 clustered in Black Rock. The city's 13,500 African Americans were still centered around the Michigan Avenue Baptist Church.

The first suburban style plaza in the area, the University Plaza, was built in 1939. It was just over the city limits on Main Street at Kenmore Avenue.

In 1945 the worst blizzard in Buffalo's history until that point hit the city. Barreling in on Christmas Eve Day, the storm buried the city in snow by nightfall. It crippled not just the city, but transportation in the entire Northeast. Railroads already bogged down by soldiers traveling for the holidays came to a standstill. The New York Central rail yard just outside the city, covered in 5 feet of snow, managed to only dig out and dispatch two trains that day, when in a normal day more than 50 departed. While certainly devastating at the time, it was just a precursor to the blizzard in 1977.

Improvements in the road system also started during this time frame. Plans for the New York State Thruway were underway by the mid 1940s, and the chosen route, while initially seen as an immense boom to the city, turned out to have severe detrimental affects on the city's neighborhoods.

BUFFALO AND THE WAR EFFORT

During the 1930s and 1940s, Buffalo's steel and aerospace industries continued to expand. While other areas of the country suffered, Buffalo prospered with more than $5 billion worth of federal war-related contracts.

With the increased need for steel for planes, tanks, and other war machines, Bethlehem-Lackawanna Steel grew to 20,000 employees, making it the largest steel plant in the world.

While the steel business boomed, the 1930s got off to an inauspicious start for the Buffalo airplane industry. After an appendix operation, Glenn Curtiss had a heart attack and died on July 23. But the firm went on without him. The firm's preeminent war aircraft, the P-40, was first tested at the corporate test field here in 1938. In 1940, the Buffalo plant had 5,300 workers. In 1941, the company opened a second plant on Genesee Street. In 1943, Curtiss-Wright built a research facility near its second plant and the number of employees had increased more than eight fold to 43,000. The various plants created nearly 17,000 planes for the war effort, primarily the 14,000-some P-40s used throughout the war from the defense of Pearl Harbor onward, including use by the Flying Tigers while protecting the Burma Road in China.

By 1945, the number of workers was back down to around 5,500. Despite efforts to convert to a civilian business, in 1946 Curtiss-Wright closed its Buffalo plants, with Plant 1 purchased by Western Electric and Plant 2 by Westinghouse. The company's aircraft research facility was donated to Cornell University, which renamed it the Cornell Aeronautical Laboratories

Also in 1930, the aerospace company Consolidated Aircraft moved to San Diego, California. The Buffalo-based general manager, Lawrence Dale Bell, stayed in town and formed his own company, Bell Aircraft, in 1935. The company designed several aircraft used later in World War II. One of the best known is the model P-39 Airacobra. First tested in 1939, the plane was sold to the RAF for its war efforts. When the United States joined the war in 1941, 600 Airacobras were already in use. Best in lower altitude combat, the plane saw use in all the World War II theaters, including Russia.

Perhaps of even more importance, however, was the P-59 Airacomet, the first American designed and built jet. Designed in total secrecy in 1942, it was tested later that year at what is now known as Andrews Air Force Base. Although only 66 P-59s were produced starting in 1943, it was a key first step in American jet design and development.

Another aviation first began in 1943 when Bell built its Model 30 helicopter. The follow-up Model 47, built in 1945, was the first commercial helicopter. In 1947, Bell Aircraft built on its jet technology by designing the X-1, which went on to earn notoriety as the aircraft flown by Chuck Yeager when he first broke the sound barrier.

To help support the war effort, local schools ran stamp programs and other fund raisers. The Fosdick-Masten High School ran two phenomenal fund raisers during the war, bringing in more than $125,000, used to "purchase" two Bell Aircraft: a $75,000 Airacobra in 1943 and a $50,000 Kingcobra in 1945.

Other war-related business booms included the motor industry and the ship building industry. General Motors opened three plants and employed nearly 90,000 workers by 1943, and two naval carriers, *Greater Buffalo* and *SeeAndBee*, were built here. The *Greater Buffalo* was originally built in Ohio in 1924 and was converted in the Buffalo shipyards to an aircraft carrier called the USS *Sable*. The *SeeAndBee*, so named after its owning company, the Cleveland and Buffalo Transit Company, was a 1913 "side-wheel excursion" ship built in Michigan. It was also converted to an aircraft carrier, commissioned as the USS *Wolverine*. The *Wolverine* was commissioned in 1942 and the *Sable* in 1943. Both served valiantly throughout the war, working as training carriers in Lake Michigan.

Unfortunately, the end of the war, which was such a boom to most areas, was devastating to Buffalo's primary industries. The post-war decline started a downward spiral that would continue through the end of the century.

Chapter Ten

THE FALL OF THE QUEEN CITY

By the mid 1900s, Buffalo had lost much of its dominance in the nation. Although the city had grown to over 500,000 people, its rank in the United States continued to decline. And, as in other areas, civic unrest and mass migration to the suburbs threatened to put an end to the city altogether.

1950s: THE BEGINNING OF THE FALL

Buffalo entered mid-century near its peak in both size and industrial dominance in the country. The 1950 population was 580,132, making the city the 14th largest in the country. The major metropolitan area, which includes all of Erie County and much of Niagara County, (the city of Buffalo, as well as the cities of Niagara Falls, North Tonawanda, Tonawanda, Lockport, Lackawanna, and 32 villages) reached nearly 1 million.

Buffalo also remained a major inland seaport and railroad hub during this decade. Thirteen railroad companies were still operating through the city, including the regional ones such as the Erie, the Lackawanna, the Lehigh Valley, the Pennsylvania, the Buffalo Creek, and the South Buffalo lines, as well as the New York Central, the Canadian National, the Pere Marquette, and the Toronto, Hamilton and Buffalo railroads.

City government experienced several firsts and lasts in this decade, starting right off in 1950 with the first Polish mayor, Joseph Murk. His inauguration ceremony was broadcast by WBEN, which was the first such broadcast on the television station that had begun operations in 1948. In July 1950, the last trolley closed and was replaced by the bus system. The last days of the Wright-designed Larkin Building were also in 1950.

Starting in 1952, several major companies moved out of town, including Spencer-Kellogg, which was the largest linseed oil company in the country, and National Aniline, the largest chemical dye company. As large companies moved out, several small companies were squeezed out of business by regional arms of large nationwide companies. One of the industries most affected by this trend was the breweries. In 1953 when Anheuser-Busch opened a distributorship, several local breweries folded.

To help improve automobile transportation in the city, the Skyway was opened in 1955, and plans were underway for the $10 million Scajaquada Expressway and the $6 million Kensington Expressway. In his 1956 State of the City address, Mayor Steven Pankow proudly asserted, "This is indeed an ambitious program. Its realization will facilitate traffic and actually refurbish our entire city. The State extends its fullest assistance in the planning and execution of these highly necessary improvements. We can look forward to a great future for our metropolis." Unfortunately, as with the Thruway, these highways ripped through prime residential areas and destroyed the fabric of the adjoining neighborhoods.

Major urban renewal projects were also in various stages of completion. These include the Masten Rehabilitation Project and the Ellicott District Project. Neither of these proved to be successful in the long term.

Perhaps most devastating to the city, however, was the 1959 opening of the St. Lawrence Seaway. Started in 1954, the Seaway connected the Great Lake ports directly to the Atlantic Ocean via the St. Lawrence River and the new Welland Canal. Thrilled with the prospect of being an international port, the citizens of Buffalo originally praised the Seaway, as it would allow larger ships to navigate the lakes more quickly.

But as the enlargement of the Sault Ste. Marie canal in the 1800s had allowed ships to bypass Cleveland and come directly to Buffalo, the Seaway allowed the ships to bypass Buffalo completely. In fact, where the canal was located, it practically forced ships to avoid the city. This killed virtually all of the remaining transhipping business in Buffalo. The decay also spread through the various shipping support services. With no market left, they folded shop or moved on to other ports.

Hardest hit were the grain-related businesses. With an ability to ship directly from Chicago and points west to Montreal, there was no need to store grain in Buffalo's huge grain elevators. There was no need for mills to remain in town, either, since other ports were now equally feasible places to conduct business.

There were some positive aspects to developments in the 1950s, though. One was the Allentown Art Festival, created in 1957. It was one of the first such events in the country and is now one of the oldest annual art festivals, but it started with a small event organized by Jason Natowitz, owner of a small business in the Allentown section of the city. Natowitz thought that an outdoor event could attract business to the struggling area and convinced some other business owners, residents, and artists that his idea could work. They formed the Allentown Village Society and organized a show, called the Buffalo Art Festival, for September that same year.

Approximately 20,000 people came into Allentown for that first event to view the works displayed by the 50-some local artists and craftspeople. Although that first event lost money, just as the Pan-American did, its "cultural success" convinced the organizers to repeat the show the following year. In 1959 the festival was held on the second weekend in June, where it has remained to this day.

The groundwork for another Buffalo institution was laid in 1959, when Mayor Frank Sedita convinced Detroit-based Ralph Wilson to bring his football franchise to Buffalo. The franchise was granted in October of 1959, and the name Bills was given to the new team that November. The season opened in 1960, playing in the War Memorial Stadium to a crowd of some 16,000 fans. Buffalo's love for and identity with this team would continue to grow throughout the rest of the century.

A little known but important national milestone in 1956 was the debut of the Cornell Safety Car, built by Liberty Mutual Insurance and Cornell Aeronautical Laboratories. This car had five windshield wipers to help keep a clear field of vision in adverse weather conditions. It also had only one door on each side; a bi-fold door folding to the rear. Perhaps most peculiar, the Safety Car had six bucket-style seats, with the drivers seat in the center of the front, not on the left. One passenger seat, facing the rear of the car, was placed directly behind the driver's seat. Other safety features in the car included steering levers instead of a steering wheel, driver armrests under the left and right steering levers to reduce the fatigue on the arms over long distance driving, and front passenger seats that slide forward and back for ease of entry.

Liberty Mutual started the safety ball rolling in 1952, partnering with Cornell because it was a pioneer in car safety research, best known today, perhaps, for its invention of the crash dummies used for the safety car research. These first two crash dummies were designed to simulate the effects of a crash on the bodies of adults and children. The adult dummy was dubbed "Thin Man," and his child-sized counterpart was called "Half Pint."

Another safety car was released in 1960 and many of its features were included in later production cars. The original 1956 car is on display in the Henry Ford Museum in Detroit.

Perhaps the most nationally significant event of the 1950s, however, was the 1959 invention of the implantable pacemaker by Buffalonian Wilson

Greatbatch. Greatbatch, a Buffalo native, was born in September 1919. He went to school in West Seneca, New York and enlisted in 1936, serving as a navy radio man during World War II. When the war was over, Greatbatch attended Cornell University, graduating in 1950 with a bachelor's degree in electrical engineering. He received his master's in electrical engineering from the University of Buffalo in 1957. As is the case with many inventions, Greatbatch was not trying to develop a pacemaker. Rather, he was trying to build a small oscillator to monitor heart beats. But he mistakenly put in the wrong resistor and the oscillator started generating electric pulses. Pacemakers had been around for quite some time prior to Greatbatch's invention, but they were large, heavy, not easily transportable devices. This gave him the idea that the device could be implanted in the body to regulate heartbeats. Greatbatch's invention would go on to save millions of lives and was named in 1985 one of the top ten inventions of the previous 50 years.

1960s: The Flight Continues

The flight of key manufacturing companies and other businesses from Buffalo continued in the 1960s. Much of this movement was because the largest businesses were no longer locally owned. They were large conglomerates formed by the merging of dozens of small businesses nationwide and their corporate managers couldn't care less about the local area. Once the financial advantages of running a Buffalo business disappeared, there was no loyalty motive to compensate for and override the profit motive.

One of the businesses to leave for Texas was Bell Aircraft. In 1961, Buffalo's only remaining shipbuilder, the American Shipbuilding Company, shut down, ending nearly 150 years of Buffalo shipbuilding starting with the *Superior* in 1821. Flour mills were also closing, with five doing so in 1966 alone.

And the state wasn't helping matters. In the early 1960s, the state was considering exempting railroads from local real property taxes. Since the New York Central Railroad was a major real estate owner in the city, this would eat further into the already shrinking tax base.

But businesses were not the only ones leaving the city. More than 80,000 city dwellers moved to the burgeoning suburbs in the 1950s. Enhancing the trend, Kensington Expressway opened in August 1967. While this exacerbated the problem, the most detrimental decision happened that same year, when the State University of New York decided to expand the school not in Buffalo but in

Amherst. Rather than helping draw school faculty, staff, and students into the city, this would force them further into the suburbs.

Buffalo's fleeing white residents were replaced largely by African Americans, whose population doubled to more than 70,000 by 1960. The urban renewal plans originally designed in the 1950s were finally put in place in the 1960s. The largest, a plan for the renewal of the Masten Park area, covered 756 acres. The Ellicott District Project was much smaller, including only 160 acres. The first of its kind in New York State, this project displaced more than 2,000 primarily African-American families. In conjunction with the federal and state plans for Buffalo development, the city of Buffalo wrote its first Master Plan during the early 1960s.

One of the most intriguing happenings of the 1960s, however, most likely went unnoticed by the city at large. In an attempt to improve traffic flow, the city implemented what is said to be the first computerized traffic signal control system in the world. It ran the traffic lights on Main Street.

A much more obvious event, on the other hand, was the National Hockey League franchise for the Buffalo Sabres, which was granted to the city in the late 1960s. The team's first season would start in 1970.

Perhaps Buffalo's most famous event, however, happened in 1964 when Frank and Teressa Bellissimo, owners of the Anchor Bar and Grill on Main Street, were asked by their son to feed a hungry mob of his friends. Teressa fried up some leftover chicken wings that usually went into the soup, Frank whipped up a spicy cayenne pepper–based sauce and covered them in it. And thus, Buffalo wings were born.

Like the industry of the time, the school system in the 1960s faced challenges. In 1965, the city school system was rated one of the least racially integrated systems in the North. The same study found that the African-American students were two to five grade levels below the rest of the students. John Curtin, federal judge, ordered the public schools integrated.

While the integration of the city schools was effective long term, it did little to ease mounting racial sentiments in the short term. Outside the African American Michigan Avenue YMCA in June 1967, rocks were thrown at the police. Then on June 27, bands of African-American teenagers started breaking the windows of the storefronts and parked cars in the William/Jefferson area. Approximately 200 police responded in full riot gear, managing to stifle the crowds with minimal damage to all parties. But the following afternoon, the outbreaks erupted again, this time with stores looted and set on fire and cars overturned. Police met this renewed activity with a force of 400. There were approximately 40 injuries in the three-day period of discontent, much lower than any of the racial outbreaks in comparable sized cities during the same period.

More discontent surfaced in 1969, but this time in regard to the Vietnam War. Draft evaders, known as the "Buffalo Nine," were arrested in a local church by federal agents.

Lest this decade look totally bereft, there were positive public and business news events in the 1960s. The most relevant to today's residents and visitors were two new corporate headquarters built on Main Street. The first, designed in 1963 and completed in 1966, was the M&T Bank Building covering the whole block from Main to Washington and Eagle to North Division. The creation of master architect Minoru Yamasaki, the 20-story white concrete building dominates the area, despite the fact that the tower on the Main Place Mall across the street is higher. This building is said to have been the prototype for Yamasaki's most impressive buildings, the former Twin Towers of the World Trade Center.

Another major bank's corporate headquarters was started in the 1960s: the Marine Midland/HSBC Center. Started in 1969, this building was not completed until 1974. Designed by Skidmore, Owings and Merrill, this 38-story building straddling Main Street is still the tallest building in the city.

The Buffalo Art Festival continued to grow throughout this decade and became formally identified with the area in which it was held in 1966 when the name of the event was officially changed to "The Allentown Outdoor Art Festival." By that time, however, the show had evolved into much more than an art show. It featured live music by groups as prestigious as the Buffalo Philharmonic Orchestra, juxtaposed with sidewalk eateries, fashion shows, even new fire trucks. From the mere 50 exhibitors in the inaugural event, the festival grew five-fold to 225 in 1961 and more than doubled again to 500 in 1968. And the exhibitors were no longer just local. Artists and craftspeople from across the United States and Canada came to display their wares, drawing more than 250,000 people to the Allentown neighborhood.

Not only was the festival good for the exhibitors, it was good for Allentown. Originally part of the farm owned by Lewis Allen, the Allentown area of downtown was settled in 1827. As the city grew north, this area developed into one of the more popular residential areas in the city, especially along the Delaware Avenue corridor. During the late 1940s and throughout the 1950s, however, this area went through a sharp decline, even though it still held some of the city's most wonderful and eclectic architecture. A large side benefit to the success of the festival was that by the late 1960s, people also began to recognize the importance of the area itself and people started moving back into Allentown.

But these new corporate buildings and a very popular annual festival alone could not stem the tide. From a peak of more than 500,000, by the end of the decade the population had gone down to 462,000.

1970s: UNWANTED NATIONAL ATTENTION

Buffalo's downward slide continued through the 1970s, although several projects were started in an attempt to halt the process. The most obvious is the Metro Rail rapid transit system. First proposed in 1973, work began on the Buffalo Metro Rail system in 1979. Designed to ease the traffic problems and parking shortage downtown, the light rail system runs from the old central wharf area to the Main Street campus of the University of Buffalo. The project costs exceeded $600 million for the 6.2-mile, 14-station, 27-car line.

Unfortunately, the project took so many years to complete that many of the businesses along its above ground section couldn't attract enough business to stay open. When it opened in 1985, it attracted less than half the anticipated ridership, primarily because there were no longer enough stores downtown to bring people in. By 1989, ridership was actually 20 percent less than bus ridership had been when the line opened.

On the city's campuses, unrest about the Vietnam War continued. In February 1970, a confrontation between students and the police led to 12 injuries, 18 arrests, and damage to nearly all the campus buildings.

The first round of layoffs at Bethlehem Steel hit in 1971. Approximately 9,000 workers were laid off, representing nearly half the work force. Two years later, Buffalo's last brewery was closed.

Sports in the city fared much better. In 1970, both the Buffalo Sabres and the Buffalo Braves played their first games in their new homes. On the other hand, in 1973, the Buffalo Bills deserted downtown, moving into their new stadium in Orchard Park. For water recreation, the Erie Basin Marina opened.

In 1976, one of the first restoration projects in the city was completed. The work on Shea's Buffalo Theater, coupled with the hopes for the new light rail, helped spur more restoration in the Theater District.

Two major hurdles for the Allentown Art Festival were successfully cleared in this decade. The first hurdle was encountered in 1970–1971. Shortly after the festival ended in 1970 a fight broke out in an Allentown bar and spread into the streets. The ensuing brawl became known as the "Allentown Art Festival Riot," and many in the city already opposed to the "carnival atmosphere" the festival had acquired called for the festival to be cancelled. Fortunately cooler heads prevailed, but the compromise molded the festival we know today. The number of exhibitors was limited to about 450, the exhibits would be juried, no crafts would be allowed, nor would any live music. These rules are still in place today.

The second Allentown hurdle occurred in 1979 when the city voted to allow local merchants to sell their wares on their sidewalks during the festival. Having just eight years earlier agreed to turn the show into a true arts venue, organizers blanched at the prospect of a flea market atmosphere likely to be promoted by the local businesses. They refused to organize a show that year until a compromise was reached allowing businesses to remain open, but not display wares on the sidewalk.

In 1978, the Allentown area, running roughly from Main to Plymouth/Cottage and from Edward through North, was designated a local historic preservation district, and in 1980, it was listed as a National Historic District on the National Register of Historic Places.

While these events affected selected Buffalonians and non-local artists, 76 years after the assassination of McKinley at the Pan-American Exposition, Buffalo again attained the national spotlight, all due to a light, fluffy, white substance known as snow. On Friday, January 28, 1977, a blizzard with 45 mile per hour winds pushing temperatures below zero hit the city, blowing around the more than 3 feet of snow still on the ground, remains from the 10 feet that had already fallen that winter.

Despite popular belief in areas outside of Buffalo, both the blizzard and the snowfall that preceeded it were rare occurances that in combination proved deadly. Seven people succumbed to the storm, but thousands were stranded in their cars and in buildings around the city. The blizzard hit at 11:35 a.m., dropping temperatures from 26 degrees to zero and increasing winds from an average of 29 miles per hour to an average of 45, with gusts of up to 75 miles per hour. The visibility dropped to zero and the wind chill factor dropped to 50–60 degrees below zero. Roads began to look like Erie Canal towpaths, then closed completely.

One of the worst calamities during the storm was the fire on Whitney Place. None of the firefighting equipment could get in, and six houses were destroyed.

But one of the most telling aspects of the episode is how the people reacted. Store, restaurant, and bar owners opened their doors and provided all the food they had at no charge. Those with snowmobiles and four wheel drive vehicles donated their time and their equipment to rush people to the hospital and bring in urgently needed medical supplies. All these things proved why another nickname for Buffalo is the "City of Good Neighbors."

The storm continued for three more days. When it finally ended on February 1, 29 people had died, more than a third frozen in their snowbound cars. Twenty animals died in the Buffalo Zoo, representing a loss of about $500,000. On a more humorous note, though, nine animals escaped, including the three reindeer who just walked out over the high drifts. Nearly 100 people were arrested for looting. Snow removal costs alone were estimated to be more than $20 million, with total costs running to more than $300 million.

The Buffalo blizzard, combined with a flood in Johnstown, Pennsylvania and fires in the Cambria mines, led to a $750 million loss that year for Bethlehem Steel. This was the first loss the company had had since the Depression, and it eventually led to the total shutdown of the Lackawanna plant in 1983.

On a more positive note, 1977 also saw the start of the Buffalo Naval and Servicemen's Park. Opened in 1979, the park is home to the USS *The Sullivans*, a destroyer, and the USS *Little Rock*, a missile cruiser. *The Sullivans* is called a Fletcher class destroyer, built in 1943 and named for the five Sullivan brothers who died on the cruiser USS *Juneau*. It is nearly 400 feet in length and nearly 40 feet wide. It is a National Historic Landmark. And for those who believe in such things, *The Sullivans* is reputed to be haunted.

The loss of Buffalo's pro basketball team, the Buffalo Braves, also came about in 1977 when the Braves moved to San Diego, California after only seven short years in the city. In 1979, however, the Buffalo Bisons, who had left the city in 1970, returned as a new AA team.

1980s: RESTORATIONS BEGIN

The decade began with one of the most spectacular man hunts in the city's history. On September 22, 1980, a black teenager, Glenn Dunn, was killed by a gunshot as he sat in a car at a supermarket. The next day, Harold Green was shot in the suburb of Cheektowaga. That same night, Emmanuel Thomas was killed back in Buffalo. On the third day, a fourth black man was shot in Niagara Falls. When police determined that all four men had been shot with the same gun, the murderer was labeled the ".22-caliber killer."

Even though the fourth murder happened in Niagara Falls, Buffalo blacks became rightfully worried that a race war was underway in the city. The fear grew when two black cabbies were found slain in their cars in early October and a third black man was nearly strangled to death in a hospital ward.

The fear gradually abated as no additional attacks occurred. Then in a surprise turn of events, six stabbings, leading to four deaths, were reported in New York City between 11:00 a.m. and midnight December 22. This killer was dubbed the "Midtown Slasher." Just one week later, another death occurred in Buffalo, this time from knife wounds, not a gun. A similar death occurred in Rochester, and three other attacks occurred through January 1, although those victims thankfully survived.

Police in both cities continued to be baffled until January 18, when a private named Joseph Christopher was arrested in Georgia for slashing a fellow soldier. In his home, police found evidence of the .22, as well as a bus ticket to New York. And his enlistment coincided with the halting of the first Buffalo murders. Christopher was convicted of the Buffalo murders, but that ruling was overturned in 1985, when he was again convicted, this time for the New York murders.

Business closings continued throughout the 1980s. The largest flour mill in the city, Standard Milling, closed its Buffalo operation in 1980. In 1982, in the midst of Buffalo's sesquicentennial, the *Courier Express* morning newspaper closed after 148 years in business. After watching Bethlehem Steel curtail its Buffalo operations in 1983, Republic Steel followed suit in 1984.

But there were some positive business moves, openings, and rebirths in the 1980s, too. Buffalo Savings Bank merged with several smaller banks into a conglomerate known as Goldome. This made it the largest thrift bank in the United States. In 1988, Pilot Field, a new downtown baseball stadium, opened and attracted record sell-out crowds in its first several years of operation. Wrapping up the decade, 1989 saw the opening of the Walden Galleria in suburban Cheektowaga. While the suburban placement of the mall was good for consumers, it had a negative impact on the already suffering downtown retail corridor. What little retail business there had been virtually stopped, because customers no longer needed to go downtown.

Two major renovations were also completed in the 1980s. In 1985, the long vacant Cyclorama Building was given new life when it was purchased for $100,000 by Frank Ciminelli and his Ciminelli Development Company. Since the building is in the Allentown National Historic District, it was eligible for tax credits as well as a variety of urban renewal grants. It took two years to negotiate the restoration details with the state, but in 1988, the bricks and mortar portion of the project finally got underway. Costing nearly $3 million, of which more than $2 million was supplied by grants and bonds, the new building opened in 1989.

The Fall of the Queen City

While the restoration of the Cyclorama was important to Buffalonians, the restoration of the Guaranty/Prudential Building in 1982 had national importance. The Guaranty Building started its slide during the Depression, and by the 1950s, its owners concluded it needed to be "modernized." As happened to many buildings in the 1950s and 1960s, the lobby ceiling was lowered and a new exterior coating given to the lobby and lower floors. Further damage was caused by sandblasting the exterior to clean it and by a 1974 fire.

The building was declared a National Historic Landmark in 1975, but the building was still losing money and no one seemed willing to buy it. By 1977, as so many naive groups do, the misguided owners decided to demolish the building so it would be easier to sell the lot. Thankfully, the outcry from Buffalonians and architecture buffs nationwide stopped the demolition. The late U.S. Senator Daniel Patrick Moynihan, always a friend to preservation, led the charge to procure funding for the restoration. The project was completed in 1982, at a cost in excess of $12 million, and one of the first new tenants was Senator Moynihan.

Still, the downward spiral throughout these years took its toll on the once great city and left many residents worried about their futures.

Chapter Eleven

THE CITY TODAY

In 1990, Buffalo's population was down to 328,123, less than in its 1901 Pan-American Exposition days, and it ranked 54th in the nation. By 2000, the population had decreased again to 292,648 and Rochester nearly passed Buffalo as the state's second largest city. But the major metropolitan area still averages about 1.2 million people and the city is starting a slow rebirth.

1990S: SPORTS FEVER

Just when Buffalonians were starting to feel more upbeat about their future, especially as an evolving mega-banking center, in 1991 the federal government shut down Goldome Savings Bank and seized its assets of more than $11 billion. Caught up in the nationwide bank problems of the 1980s, Goldome just couldn't recover. Although Key Bank and M&T Bank split Goldome's branches, the loss of local jobs was still significant.

The years 1991 through 1994 were marred by a different type of agony. The Buffalo Bills football team made it into the Super Bowl for four consecutive years, then managed to lose all four games. The entire city and surrounding areas as far east as Rochester were in a frenzy over the first 1991 trip to the Super Bowl. Slated to play Super Bowl XXV against the New York Giants in Tampa, everyone thought that a Bills win was a shoo-in. Although the prospects looked good, fate was not to be kind. With a score of 20 to 19, Bills kicker Scott Norwood missed the winning field goal wide right. While Norwood took the brunt of the loss, and is still castigated for his role, a closer look at the game shows that 5 of those 19 losing points were made by Norwood. It certainly was not his fault the Bills lost; it was the entire team's and the fans need to stop blaming the man.

Unfortunately, that first attempt was the only one of the four to be remotely close. The Bills lost Super Bowl XXVI to the Washington Redskins in Minneapolis by a score of 34 to 27. Quarterback Jim Kelly managed to throw four interceptions in that game, but he never bore the brunt of criticism that Norwood did after the first loss.

BUFFALO

In 1993, the Bills won their league again and faced the Dallas Cowboys in Super Bowl XXVII held in the Rose Bowl in Pasadena. Managing their worst loss, the Bills scored only 17 points to the Cowboy's 52. Again in 1994, the Bills won the AFC and were matched with the Cowboys for Super Bowl XXVIII. Playing in the Georgia Dome in Atlanta, the Bills lost for the fourth time with a final score of 30 to 13.

While the fans are right to be disappointed, and critics have some justification in pointing out the team's poor showings, especially in the three latter games, what everyone seems to forget is that the Buffalo Bills are the only team in NFL history to make it to the Super Bowl in four consecutive years—a record not likely to be broken any time soon.

During this same time frame, however, Buffalo not only generated positive press but enhanced its sports facilities, all in preparation for hosting the 1993 World University Games. Founded in 1923 for university athletic competition, the World University Games have summer and winter events, just like the Olympics. The Buffalo games were the first and only time the event was held in the United States. Buffalo's participation as a venue was garnered by local businessman Burt Flickinger, who persuaded the games officials to take a chance on the city. Running July 6–18, the World University Games attracted in excess of 5,000 athletes from more than 100 countries.

While the games lost money just like the Pan-American did, they had equally long-lasting positive effects. First, the temperatures for the games were among the hottest in the city's history and helped shatter our image as a snowbound wasteland. Second, the facilities built for the games continue to attract additional sporting events. The 18,000 seat stadium at the University of Buffalo is used for the school's own games, but also for other events. It is estimated that the Olympic pool in the Burt Flickinger Athletic Center at Erie County Community College's city campus has generated nearly $50 million in revenues.

Later in 1993, via the creation of the Buffalo Free-Net, Buffalo was one of the first cities in the country to provide free internet access to its citizens. Though founded in 1992, the service officially opened in October 1993. The Buffalo Free-Net still provides free hosting services to local charitable and special interest groups, including one of the first genealogy websites in the country.

In 1994, another sporting venue opened, the Marine Midland Arena. Home to the Buffalo Sabres hockey team, the arena also was the site for basketball games, concerts, and other events. The name was changed to HSBC Arena in 1999 when Marine Midland changed its name to HSBC Bank USA.

The city saw the reincarnation of one of its major cultural attractions also in 1994. After a series of donations from Dr. Charles Penney, the name of the Burchfield Art Center was changed to the Burchfield-Penney Art Center. Located on the campus of Buffalo State College, just across Elmwood from the world famous Albright-Knox Art Gallery, the Burchfield-Penney is another significant force in the city's fame in art circles.

Originally founded in 1966 as the Charles Burchfield Museum, the center displays the works of Burchfield, and encourages the development of art skills and knowledge in the area's residents. Charles Burchfield was born in 1893 in Ohio and moved to Buffalo in 1921 to work as a designer in George Birge's wallpaper firm. He started showing his paintings in New York City in 1929 and was soon able to support himself and his family on his artwork sales. Throughout the 1930s and 1940s, Burchfield developed a name for himself with his realistic watercolor images of life on Buffalo's streets. The 1994 name change is fitting, as Penney's donations to the center included his entire collection of works by Charles Burchfield, which at that time was the largest private collection of Burchfield art in the world.

Three years later, two expansions helped renew the city's vigor. The new, award-winning terminal at the Buffalo Niagara International Airport opened in 1997. That same year, Roswell Park Institute, one of the major cancer research and treatment centers in the world, opened its greatly expanded facilities.

In 1998, the company that owned the Guaranty Building went bankrupt, and the future of the National Historic Landmark was again threatened. In 2002, however, Hodgson Russ LLP, one of the city's largest law firms, purchased the building and is in the process of consolidating all of its Buffalo offices into the grand structure.

TODAY

In the past decade, Buffalo seems to have started a slow crawl out of its hole. It's true that the city's population has continued to decline, but this statistic is deceptive. While the number of people living in the city has definitely decreased, the total number of people in the major metropolitan area has remained relatively stable. There is a push in the area toward regional government, which, if enacted, would help stabilize the city as well as the suburban areas.

There has been redevelopment in the city center and somewhat along the waterfront, especially in the old manufacturing brownfields. They are being reclaimed and reused.

BUFFALO

In an attempt to get some of this jump-started, several new groups dedicated to the city's rebirth have formed. These include The New Millennium Group, the Buffalo-Niagara Partnership, and the Buffalo Campaign for Architecture, History, and Culture. Joining the existing Landmark Society of the Niagara Frontier and the Preservation Coalition of Erie County, these groups are focusing on building on Buffalo's history as a basis for the city's renaissance.

The Allentown Art Festival is also doing its share in bringing vitality and recognition to the city. The two day event continues to draw upwards of 450,000 people downtown each year, and in 2000, it was recognized by the Library of Congress as one of approximately 1,300 events nationwide deemed important enough to a community to be dubbed a "Local Legacy."

Most importantly, heart is returning to the city. Neighbors are banding together in block clubs, bicycling groups, and other forward-looking organizations fighting to restore what has been lost. These groups are helping to stabilize the city one neighborhood at a time.

Major renovation projects are underway at Frank Lloyd Wright's Darwin Martin complex and at Graycliff. Discussions are being held on how to restore Richardson's Psychiatric Center and the abandoned Central Terminal. There are proposals for extending the light rail system to the airport, as well as for the reconstruction of the Erie Canal central wharf and surrounding areas.

Shortly after the Erie Canal opened, an avid Buffalo fan stated, "Buffalo has no rival—it can have none. Cities west of us may arise to wealth and importance, but they will be our tributaries; . . . thus rendering Buffalo what it may ever claim to be—the Great National Exchange." This has proven true. While the city itself has seen cycles of prosperity and depression, all the great western cities do owe their existence to Buffalo.

It is fitting, then, that she remains one of only four cities in the country with architectural and cultural treasures by the recognized master architects in the world. But it is not just the Buffalo work of the trinity of Sullivan, Wright, and Richardson; it is also the supporting cast that makes Buffalo unique. In a 1991 breakthrough book on master architects, Roxanne Williamson lists 236 architects generally considered to be masters. She divides them into three groups based on when they practiced. There are 167 in the era born before 1875, 43 in the 1875 to 1905 era, and 26 born after 1905 and before 1926. Within the first tier that includes Richardson, *et al*, Buffalo has had buildings designed by five of the top five architects. We have 7 of the top 15, 14 of the top 35, and 23 of the 140. More importantly, the work of all but two of these 23 is still extant.

The City Today

In the second group, we have buildings by two of the top ten and three of the top 20. Most surprising, however, are the numbers for the contemporary masters. We have buildings by three of the top five and five of the top fifteen. This means that we have works by 29 recognized architectural masters as well as the hundreds of locally significant buildings designed by the leading Buffalo architects. Proper planning, capitalizing on this architectural legacy, and focusing on the city's strong sense of neighborhood communities will keep Buffalo "The City of Good Neighbors." It will also return Buffalo to her rightful place as Queen City of the Lakes.

BIBLIOGRAPHY

Allen, Lewis F. *First appearance, in 1832, of the cholera in Buffalo*. Buffalo: Buffalo Historical Society, 1891 (as read before the society in 1869).

Ball, Sheldon. *Buffalo in 1825*. Buffalo: Buffalo Historical Society, reprinted from a pamphlet published 1825.

Barton, James L. "Early reminiscences of Buffalo and vicinity." Read before the Buffalo Historical Society, 1866.

Bryant, William C. "Orlando Allen; Glimpses of life in the village of Buffalo." Read before the Buffalo Historical Society, 1877.

Dart, Joseph. "The grain elevators of Buffalo." Read before the Buffalo Historical Society, 1865.

Dunn, Walter S. *History of Erie County, 1870–1970*. Buffalo: Buffalo and Erie County Historical Society, 1972.

Fox, Austin M. *Church tales of the Niagara Frontier: legend, history & architecture Buffalo*. Buffalo: Western New York Wares, Inc., 1994.

French, J. H. *Gazetteer of the State of New York: embracing a comprehensive view of the geography, geology, and general history of the state, and a complete history and description of every county, city, town, village, and locality*. Syracuse: R.P. Smith, 1860.

Ketchum, William. "The origin of the name of Buffalo." Read before the Buffalo Historical Society, 1863.

Kowsky, Francis R. *Buffalo architecture: a guide*. Boston: MIT Press, 1981.

Landon, Joseph. *Notes of Joseph Landon, a surveyor who reached Buffalo Creek in 1796, and settled here in 1806*. Buffalo: Buffalo Historical Society, 1879 (as read before the society in 1863).

Leary, Thomas E. and Elizabeth C. Sholes. *From fire to rust: business, technology, and work at the Lackawanna Steel Plant, 1900-1983*. Buffalo: Buffalo and Erie County Historical Society, 1987.

Lord, John C. "Samuel Wilkeson." Read before the Buffalo Historical Society, 1871.

Lossing, Benson J. *Pictorial Field-book of the War of 1812*. New York: Harper and Brothers, 1868.

Mingus, Nancy Blumenstalk. "John Hopper Coxhead: the client connections." Unpublished thesis, Goucher College, Buffalo, 2001.

Mueller, Jacob E. *Buffalo and Its German Community*. Buffalo: German-American Historical and Biographical Society, 1912. Translated by Susan Kriegbaum-Hanks and available on line at www.archivaria.com.

BUFFALO

Napora, James. "Houses of worship: a guide to the religious architecture of Buffalo, New York." Unpublished thesis, University at Buffalo, Buffalo, 1995.

Rizzo, Michael. *Through The Mayor's Eyes.* www.buffalonian.com/history/industry/mayors/

Severance, Frank H. *The Picture Book of Earlier Buffalo.* Buffalo: Buffalo Historical Society, 1912.

Whitford, Noble E. *History of the Canal System Of the State of New York Together with Brief Histories of the Canals Of the United States and Canada.* Albany: Brandow Printing Company, 1906.

Wilner, Morton M. *Niagara frontier; a narrative and documentary history.* Chicago: The S.J. Clarke Publishing Co., 1931.

INDEX

Adam, James Noble, 124

African-American immigrants, 47, 50, 115, 126

Albright Art Gallery, 61, 107, 153

Bell Aircraft, 137, 142

Bethune, Louise, 107, 108

Black Rock, 14, 23, 25, 27–29, 31–34, 40, 45, 49, 52, 97, 136

blizzards, 136, 146, 147

breweries, 27, 41, 42, 44, 59, 60, 62, 140, 145

Buffalo Creek, 9–11, 14–16, 19, 20, 29, 33, 34, 38, 57, 139

Buffalo wings, 143

Burnham, Daniel, 104, 107, 119

Burning 1813, 23, 24, 28, 33, 64

Carrier, Willis, 110

Chapin, Cyrenius, 20, 25, 38

cholera, 38–40, 52, 58

Clemens, Samuel, 53

Cleveland, Grover, 51–53

Clinton, Dewitt, 31, 32, 36

Cornell Safety Car, 141

Curtiss, Glenn, 123, 131, 136

Dart, Joseph, 43, 44, 59

Dorsheimer, Philip, 42, 48, 55

Eidlitz, Cyrus, 56, 97

Ellicott, Joseph, 13, 17–20, 31–33, 38, 104

Ellicott Square, 104, 105, 106

Erie Canal, 31, 33, 35, 40, 42, 49, 57, 58, 126, 146, 154

Erie County Savings Bank, 62, 106

Esenwein and Johnson, 61, 107, 109, 112, 123

Fillmore, Millard, 48, 51–53

Fitch Creche, 99, 104

Grand Army of the Republic (GAR), 111, 118

German immigrants, 41, 42, 46, 50, 126

grain elevators, 43, 59, 64, 140

Granger, Erastus, 20, 23, 26, 51

Greatbatch, Wilson, 141, 142

Green, Edward B., 106, 107, 112

The *Griffon*, 14

Guaranty/Prudential building, 104–106, 149, 153

harbor, 21, 28, 29, 33–38, 40, 43, 59, 131, 132, 134

Hennepin, Father, 14

Hodges, Joe, 15

Holland Purchase, 17–19, 42

incorporation, 23, 24, 31, 39, 40, 98

Italian immigrants, 50

Johnson, William, 15, 20, 21

Kleinhans Music Hall, 133

La Salle, Rene Robert Cavelier de, 13, 14

Lackawanna Steel, 123, 131, 132, 136, 147

Lafayette Square, 56, 107, 124

Landon, Joseph, 15, 16, 21, 22, 23

Lane, Ezekiel, 15, 16, 19, 20

Larkin, John D., 62, 105, 106

Larkin Soap Company, 62, 105, 106

lighthouse, 21, 29, 43

Manufacturers and Traders Trust, 62

Masten Park High School, 109

McKinley, President William, 107, 111–113, 117–120, 125, 147

Middaugh, Martin, 11, 15, 16, 19, 20, 22

Milburn, John, 113, 118, 119, 132

Native Americans, 9–11, 13–15, 17–19

New Amsterdam, 11, 19

Olmsted, Frederick Law, 52, 54–56, 61, 106

Pan-American Exposition, 63, 107, 109, 111, 113–121, 123, 125, 128, 132, 141, 146, 151, 152

Pierce, Dr. Ray Vaughn, 62

Pierce-Arrow Motor Company, 63, 127–130

Polish immigrants, 50, 52, 100

Porter, Peter Buell, 30–34

Post, George, 104, 106

railroads, 35, 37, 40, 44, 45, 49, 50, 53, 57–59, 63, 103, 108, 112, 113, 126, 134, 136, 139, 142

Ransom, Asa, 15, 17

Richardson, H.H., 55, 56, 106, 154

Roosevelt, Theodore, 113, 118, 119, 129

Saarinan, Eliel and Eero, 134

St. Paul's Church, 47, 54, 106

Sullivan, Louis, 104–106, 154

Thomas Motor Car Company, 130

Timon, Bishop John, 41, 98–100

Walden, Ebenezer, 21–25, 35

Walk-in-the-Water, 28, 29

Wilkeson, Samuel, 24, 34–36, 39

Winney, Cornelius, 10, 14, 15

Wright, Frank Lloyd, 104–106, 139, 154

YMCA, 98, 124, 126, 143

Zoological Gardens, 61